The Metaverse Developer's Handbook

Designing Virtual Worlds
Understand the tools,
platforms, and business of
the metaverse

THOMPSON CARTER

Table of Content

TABLE OF CONTENTS

INTRODUCTION

The Metaverse Developer's Handbook: Designing Virtual Worlds

The Metaverse is no longer a distant dream; it's a rapidly growing digital reality. Imagine a universe where the virtual and physical worlds seamlessly blend, where users can interact, socialize, work, play, and even create entire economies in immersive, interconnected virtual environments. This is the promise of the **Metaverse**—a sprawling, digital universe that allows people to transcend the limitations of physical space and time, enabling new ways to experience life, work, and entertainment.

With major tech companies like Meta (formerly Facebook), Google, and Microsoft investing heavily in the Metaverse, its potential to revolutionize how we engage with digital environments is becoming clearer every day. From virtual reality (VR) experiences to augmented reality (AR), blockchain-based digital assets, and decentralized economies, the Metaverse is set to change how we interact with the world around us.

At the heart of the Metaverse lies the need for skilled developers—those who can build the virtual worlds, design interactive experiences, and shape the technologies that will define this new digital frontier. If you're someone who wants to be part of this revolution, you've come to the right place. This book, **The Metaverse Developer's Handbook: Designing Virtual Worlds**, is your guide to entering the world of Metaverse development. Whether you're a seasoned developer or a newcomer eager to learn, this book will provide you with the knowledge and tools needed to build the virtual worlds of tomorrow.

The Promise and Potential of the Metaverse

The Metaverse is not just a technological trend—it's an entirely new way of interacting with the digital world. Encompassing virtual spaces, augmented reality experiences, digital economies, and interconnected online communities, the Metaverse provides a unique opportunity to create immersive environments where users can explore, interact, and even build their own digital realities.

But with such vast potential comes the need for robust development skills and creative thinking. Developers are the architects of the Metaverse, designing the spaces, tools, and interactions that will make it an engaging and sustainable environment. From building virtual homes and offices to designing entire cities, the demand for innovative virtual world designers is growing exponentially.

Why This Book?

While the concept of the Metaverse might sound like a far-off dream, it's already becoming a reality. The increasing accessibility of VR, AR, blockchain, and AI technologies has paved the way for developers to create more immersive and interconnected virtual spaces than ever before. But for those eager to dive into Metaverse development, the question becomes: **where do you start?**

That's where this book comes in. **The Metaverse Developer's Handbook** is designed to take you on a comprehensive journey through the various aspects of Metaverse development, from understanding the foundational technologies to mastering the tools and platforms used by today's leading virtual world creators. Whether you're building your first 3D game or creating a fully immersive social space, this book provides the roadmap for success.

In these pages, you will learn the core principles of Metaverse development, including:

- **Virtual World Design**: From basic principles of designing engaging virtual spaces to advanced techniques in 3D modeling, this book covers the strategies and best practices that make virtual worlds feel immersive and dynamic.

- **Game Engines and Development Tools**: You'll gain a deep understanding of the tools used to build virtual worlds, such as **Unity**, **Unreal Engine**, and **Roblox Studio**, and learn how to leverage these platforms to bring your ideas to life.

- **Programming and Scripting**: Learn the essential coding languages (like **C#** for Unity and **Blueprints** for Unreal Engine) and scripting techniques that will enable you to create interactive environments, AI-driven NPCs, and multiplayer experiences in the Metaverse.

- **Blockchain Integration**: As blockchain technologies continue to evolve, learn how to integrate **NFTs**, **cryptocurrencies**, and **smart contracts** into your virtual worlds, allowing for the creation and trading of digital assets.

- **Monetization and Business Models**: The Metaverse is also an emerging market, with ample opportunities for developers to monetize their creations. This book will walk you through different monetization strategies, including virtual goods sales, in-game economies, and real estate investments.

- **Ethical and Societal Considerations**: As we build virtual worlds, we must also consider the ethical and societal implications. This book will touch on important issues such as **data privacy**, **economic inequality**, and the impact of digital addiction, giving you the tools to create responsible and inclusive virtual environments.

Who Is This Book For?

This book is written for anyone who wants to get involved in the development of virtual worlds and the Metaverse. Whether you're an aspiring game developer, a digital artist, or someone with a passion for technology and innovation, this book provides a comprehensive guide to mastering the skills necessary for Metaverse development.

- **Beginners**: If you're new to development or 3D design, this book will introduce you to the key concepts and tools used in the Metaverse, breaking down complex topics into accessible lessons.

- **Intermediate Developers**: If you have some experience in game development or virtual environments, this book will deepen your understanding of Metaverse-specific technologies and help you build more complex, interactive virtual worlds.

- **Experienced Creators and Entrepreneurs**: If you're already building in the Metaverse or working in VR/AR development, this book will provide valuable insights into the business side of Metaverse creation, from monetization strategies to cross-platform integration.

What You'll Learn in This Book

This book is divided into several sections, each designed to equip you with the knowledge and skills to succeed in Metaverse development:

1. **Introduction to the Metaverse**: Understand what the Metaverse is, its history, and how it's evolving. Learn about the technologies that power the Metaverse, such as **VR**, **AR**, **blockchain**, and **AI**.

2. **Designing Virtual Worlds**: Learn the principles of immersive virtual world design, including 3D modeling, spatial design, user avatars, and the importance of interaction and engagement.

3. **Developing Virtual Worlds**: Dive into the tools and technologies needed to create virtual environments. Learn to use game engines like **Unity** and **Unreal Engine**, and gain hands-on experience with platforms like **Roblox** and **Decentraland**.

4. **Creating Multiplayer and Social Experiences**: Explore how to build social interactions, multiplayer systems, and AI-driven behaviors within your virtual worlds.

5. **Blockchain and Digital Assets**: Discover how blockchain technology is used in the Metaverse, including the creation and management of **NFTs**, **virtual currencies**, and **smart contracts**.

6. **Business Models in the Metaverse**: Understand the economic opportunities within the Metaverse, including **monetization** strategies, **virtual real estate**, and **digital goods** sales.

7. **Ethical and Societal Considerations**: Delve into the ethical challenges of the Metaverse, including **privacy**, **economic inequality**, and **mental health**

concerns, and learn how to create responsible virtual spaces.

8. **Getting Involved in the Metaverse Community**: Learn how to connect with other developers, share your work, and contribute to the growth of the Metaverse.

Conclusion: A New Frontier for Developers

The Metaverse is still in its infancy, but it's growing at an exponential rate. As more businesses, communities, and users enter this digital universe, the demand for skilled developers will only increase. Whether you're interested in creating the next big game, building a virtual social platform, or developing a thriving virtual economy, the Metaverse offers limitless opportunities for innovation and creativity.

This book is your gateway to understanding and mastering the skills necessary for Metaverse development. It will guide you through the tools, technologies, and strategies you need to succeed in this exciting new field. So, if you're ready to be part of the next evolution of the internet, the Metaverse is waiting for you.

Let's build the future, one virtual world at a time.

CHAPTER 1

WHAT IS THE METAVERSE?

Overview: Define the Metaverse and Explore Its Origins

The term "Metaverse" has gained significant traction in recent years, particularly with the rise of virtual worlds and immersive technologies. At its core, the Metaverse refers to a collective, interconnected virtual environment that blends digital spaces, augmented reality (AR), virtual reality (VR), and real-world interactions. It is an expansive, immersive universe where users can interact with each other and digital environments through avatars, exchange virtual goods, and participate in social, economic, and creative activities.

The concept of the Metaverse isn't new; its roots trace back to science fiction, notably to Neal Stephenson's 1992 novel *Snow Crash*. In the novel, the Metaverse was a virtual world accessed by users through avatars and used for everything from business meetings to entertainment. This vision of a connected, immersive virtual world captured the imagination of many and set the stage for real-world attempts to build similar environments.

The Metaverse has evolved beyond the confines of science fiction to become a real technological and cultural phenomenon. It is the convergence of several key technologies:

- **Virtual Reality (VR)**: Fully immersive digital environments that users can explore through VR headsets.

- **Augmented Reality (AR)**: A technology that overlays digital content onto the real world, typically viewed through smartphones or AR glasses.

- **Blockchain**: A decentralized digital ledger technology that facilitates secure, transparent transactions and the creation of virtual assets like NFTs (Non-Fungible Tokens).

- **Social Interactions**: Real-time, online interactions where users engage with one another, similar to how we communicate and collaborate in the real world.

The Metaverse integrates all these elements, creating a space where digital and physical realities converge. It is not limited to games or entertainment; it includes a variety of experiences, from virtual meetings and shopping to virtual real estate and education.

Real-world Example: Comparing Early Metaverse Concepts to Modern VR Platforms

To better understand the Metaverse, let's look at how the concept has evolved over time, comparing early virtual worlds to modern VR platforms.

Second Life: The Early Vision of the Metaverse

- **Origin**: Launched in 2003, *Second Life* was one of the earliest and most ambitious attempts at creating an online virtual world that resembled the Metaverse. It was a fully immersive 3D world where users could create avatars, build structures, develop virtual businesses, and socialize in real time.

- **User Interactions**: In *Second Life*, users had the ability to interact with each other, purchase virtual land, create virtual goods, and participate in a wide range of activities, from gaming to attending concerts. The economy in *Second Life* was supported by a virtual currency called the Linden Dollar, which had real-world value.

- **Key Features**:
  - **Customization**: Users could fully customize their avatars and the virtual spaces they inhabited.
  - **User-Generated Content**: One of the defining aspects of *Second Life* was its emphasis on user-generated content. Users could create their own virtual environments, clothing, objects, and experiences.
  - **Limitations**: While *Second Life* was groundbreaking in many ways, it had limitations in terms of graphics quality, real-time interactions, and immersive experiences. Its user base also faced barriers related to the complex

user interface and limited integration with other platforms.

Modern VR Platforms: Facebook's Horizon Worlds

- **Overview**: Facebook (now Meta) launched *Horizon Worlds* as a modern iteration of the Metaverse concept. Unlike *Second Life*, which was primarily a 2D platform that users accessed through desktops, *Horizon Worlds* is designed for immersive VR experiences, where users can interact in real-time in fully realized 3D virtual environments.

- **User Interactions**: In *Horizon Worlds*, users can create and customize avatars, build virtual environments, play games, attend events, and interact with friends in real time. The platform supports multiplayer experiences and offers tools for users to create their own virtual spaces, games, and experiences. The integration of VR makes the platform more immersive and interactive compared to its predecessors.

- **Key Features**:
  - **Fully Immersive VR**: Unlike *Second Life*, *Horizon Worlds* is fully immersive, designed to be experienced with VR headsets like Oculus. This means users can navigate the space more naturally, with 360-degree views and real-time body movements.

- o **Social Interactions**: Much like *Second Life*, *Horizon Worlds* emphasizes social interaction, but with the added benefit of being in VR, which allows for more lifelike and engaging interactions between avatars.

- o **Cross-Platform Integration**: *Horizon Worlds* integrates with Facebook's broader ecosystem, enabling seamless social experiences across the platform. Users can also interact with Facebook friends and discover events and activities through the app.

- o **Economy and Transactions**: Similar to the Linden Dollar in *Second Life*, *Horizon Worlds* has its own economy, where creators can monetize their content. Facebook's push toward cryptocurrency and the integration of blockchain into the Metaverse is likely to shape the virtual economy of platforms like *Horizon Worlds* in the future.

The Evolution of the Metaverse: Key Differences Between Second Life and Horizon Worlds

- **Platform Type**: *Second Life* was primarily a PC-based platform accessed via a desktop or laptop, while *Horizon*

Worlds is fully immersive and requires a VR headset. This shift represents a significant evolution in terms of user experience, moving from 2D interactions to 3D, immersive environments.

- **Interactivity and Engagement**: *Horizon Worlds* offers more interactive experiences compared to *Second Life*. In *Second Life*, user interactions were more focused on chatting, building, and creating within a virtual world, while *Horizon Worlds* incorporates a deeper sense of presence through VR, making interactions feel more personal and lifelike.

- **Economic Integration**: Both platforms have economies where virtual goods and services can be traded, but *Horizon Worlds* is more deeply integrated with Meta's social ecosystem, paving the way for a future where users can create, buy, and sell digital assets seamlessly across various platforms.

- **Social Features**: *Horizon Worlds* emphasizes social interaction in a way that *Second Life* did not, with a focus on real-time interaction using avatars, games, and social spaces. This aligns with Meta's broader vision of creating a fully interconnected social Metaverse, where virtual worlds, social interactions, and commerce converge.

Conclusion

The Metaverse, while still in its early stages, represents the next frontier in the digital landscape. From the origins of *Second Life* as a virtual world based on user-generated content to the cutting-edge VR experiences of *Horizon Worlds*, the Metaverse has evolved significantly. As technologies such as VR, AR, blockchain, and AI continue to advance, the Metaverse will only become more immersive, interconnected, and integrated into daily life.

As developers, designers, and businesses look to build within this new virtual space, understanding its roots, technologies, and potential applications is essential. The Metaverse offers immense opportunities for innovation, and this book will guide you through the process of designing and building in this exciting new frontier.

CHAPTER 2

THE HISTORY AND EVOLUTION OF VIRTUAL WORLDS

Overview: Discuss the Progression from Early Text-Based Environments (Like MUDs) to Graphical MMOs (Massively Multiplayer Online Games) and Current VR/AR Experiences

Virtual worlds have evolved significantly over the past few decades, transforming from simple text-based games to the immersive, lifelike experiences we see today. The Metaverse, which is often associated with cutting-edge VR (Virtual Reality) and AR (Augmented Reality) environments, has its roots in early text-based systems, graphical MMOs, and multiplayer games that paved the way for more sophisticated virtual spaces.

In this chapter, we'll look at the historical development of virtual worlds and explore how these environments have evolved over time, starting with the early days of text-based games to the current immersive VR and AR experiences. By tracing this evolution, we can better understand the technologies, user experiences, and design principles that have shaped modern virtual worlds and the Metaverse.

1. The Early Days: Text-Based Virtual Worlds and MUDs

In the late 1970s and 1980s, the first virtual worlds began to take shape as text-based environments that allowed users to interact with each other through written commands and descriptions. These worlds were typically hosted on early mainframe computers and accessed via command-line interfaces. The most significant example of this early era was the **Multi-User Dungeon (MUD)**, which was first developed in 1978.

- **MUDs (Multi-User Dungeons)**: MUDs were the first true virtual worlds, allowing multiple players to explore fantasy settings, solve puzzles, engage in combat, and interact with one another through typed commands. Players would explore "rooms" in the game, each described through text, and could communicate with each other via chat.
  - **Real-world Example**: A player might type the command "look" to get a description of the room they were in, such as "You are standing in a dark forest. There is a path to the north and a cave entrance to the east."
  - **Legacy**: MUDs paved the way for all subsequent multiplayer experiences by introducing the concept of real-time, shared digital spaces where users could socialize, play, and collaborate.

- **Text-Based Adventure Games**: Alongside MUDs, text-based adventure games like *Zork* (1977) and *Adventure* (1976) allowed players to explore worlds described entirely in text, solving puzzles and interacting with their environment. Though these games were single-player experiences, they helped shape the structure and mechanics of modern virtual worlds.

While these early systems lacked the graphical fidelity we expect today, they provided the foundation for interaction, socialization, and exploration within virtual spaces.

2. The Rise of Graphical MMOs: The 1990s and Early 2000s

As computing power increased and internet access became more widespread, the 1990s marked a significant shift in virtual worlds, with the introduction of **graphical MMOs (Massively Multiplayer Online Games)**. These games introduced graphics, allowing players to experience digital worlds through avatars instead of text descriptions. These MMOs took the multiplayer and exploration aspects of MUDs and turned them into fully immersive 3D environments.

- **Early Graphical MMOs**: Games like *Meridian 59* (1996) and *The Realm Online* (1996) were among the first to offer a graphical representation of the virtual world. However, it was the release of *EverQuest* (1999) that truly changed the landscape of online gaming, setting the stage for the massive success of future MMOs.

- **World of Warcraft (WoW)**: *World of Warcraft*, released in 2004, became the defining game in the MMO genre. With millions of players online simultaneously, *WoW* created a vast, persistent online world where users could explore, fight monsters, complete quests, and socialize in real-time. The game featured an open world with diverse environments, from lush forests to icy tundras, and allowed players to form guilds, engage in player-vs-environment (PvE) content, and participate in large-scale player-vs-player (PvP) battles.

  - **Real-world Example**: *World of Warcraft* allowed players to create and customize avatars, team up for group quests, trade virtual goods, and even form long-lasting friendships. This social aspect became a major draw, with players spending hours in-game for both the gameplay and the social interactions.

  - **Legacy**: *WoW* and other MMOs like *Final Fantasy XIV* and *Guild Wars 2* shaped many of the design principles in modern virtual worlds, such as persistent worlds, quest-based progression, and in-game economies.

The success of MMOs in the 2000s demonstrated the power of virtual worlds to engage players, creating spaces where people could live out fantasy adventures, work together, and build communities.

3. The Evolution Toward Virtual Reality (VR) and Augmented Reality (AR)

In the 2010s, as VR and AR technologies matured, the concept of virtual worlds evolved again, with the introduction of fully immersive environments where users could experience virtual spaces through VR headsets and AR devices.

- **Virtual Reality (VR)**: Early attempts at VR in the 1990s, such as the *Virtual Boy* by Nintendo and *SEGA VR*, were limited by technological constraints. However, with the release of Oculus Rift in 2016 and the rapid advancements in VR hardware, immersive VR platforms became more accessible to the average consumer.
  - o **Real-world Example**: *Oculus Rift* and *HTC Vive* offered fully immersive experiences where players could interact with virtual worlds through

26

headsets, controllers, and even haptic feedback devices. VR platforms like *VRChat* became popular for their social interaction features, allowing users to meet and chat in virtual spaces, create avatars, and explore user-generated environments.

- **Augmented Reality (AR)**: Unlike VR, which creates entirely virtual environments, AR overlays digital content onto the real world. The success of AR applications like *Pokémon Go* (2016), which allowed players to capture virtual Pokémon in real-world locations, demonstrated the potential of AR to create shared experiences that blend digital and physical realities.

    o **Real-world Example**: *Pokémon Go* allowed players to use their mobile devices to explore their surroundings and interact with virtual objects. This marked a significant shift toward integrating digital experiences into everyday life, showcasing the potential of AR in the Metaverse.

4. The Convergence of Virtual Worlds and the Metaverse

Today, we are beginning to see the convergence of VR, AR, blockchain, and social interaction within a unified vision of the Metaverse—a collective, interconnected virtual universe where users can move between different virtual spaces, socialize, work, and play.

- **The Vision for the Metaverse**: The Metaverse aims to bring together elements from all these technologies, allowing users to seamlessly move between virtual and augmented environments. Major tech companies, such as Facebook (now Meta), Microsoft, and Epic Games, are investing heavily in Metaverse-related technologies, with the goal of creating interconnected virtual worlds that users can navigate and interact with in real-time.

  - **Real-world Example**: Meta's *Horizon Worlds* is a VR platform that allows users to interact in shared virtual spaces, create content, play games, and socialize with friends and strangers alike. The platform is an example of how VR, social interaction, and virtual commerce are beginning to intersect in the Metaverse.

The Metaverse is no longer a concept confined to science fiction. It is becoming a reality as VR, AR, and other technologies continue to evolve. As developers, designers, and entrepreneurs, the challenge now is to build these interconnected virtual worlds and create experiences that are engaging, immersive, and accessible to all.

Conclusion

The evolution of virtual worlds—from the early text-based environments like MUDs to the fully immersive VR/AR experiences of today—has been marked by a steady increase in user interaction, graphical fidelity, and immersive technologies. The development of MMOs in the late 90s and early 2000s laid the foundation for modern virtual worlds, and the rise of VR and AR technologies in the 2010s has pushed the concept of the Metaverse to the forefront of the tech industry.

The Metaverse, as we understand it today, is a culmination of these advancements, blending VR, AR, blockchain, and social interaction into a cohesive virtual universe. As this space continues to evolve, the opportunities for developers to create new virtual experiences, economies, and communities will only expand, offering exciting prospects for both the digital and physical worlds.

In the following chapters, we will explore the tools, platforms, and technologies that are shaping this new frontier, providing you with the knowledge needed to design and develop for the Metaverse.

CHAPTER 3

KEY TECHNOLOGIES BEHIND THE METAVERSE

Overview: Break Down the Core Technologies That Enable the Metaverse

The Metaverse is a multi-faceted concept that combines various emerging technologies to create a seamless and immersive digital experience. It is not a single platform but rather a convergence of technologies that allow users to interact, create, and socialize in virtual environments that feel more like the physical world. While the Metaverse is still evolving, certain key technologies form its backbone, driving its growth and defining its potential.

In this chapter, we will explore the core technologies that enable the Metaverse, including **Virtual Reality (VR)**, **Augmented Reality (AR)**, **Blockchain**, **Artificial Intelligence (AI)**, and **Cloud Computing**. Each of these technologies plays a pivotal role in shaping the future of virtual worlds and providing users with immersive, interactive, and decentralized experiences.

1. Virtual Reality (VR) and Augmented Reality (AR)

Virtual Reality (VR) and **Augmented Reality (AR)** are two technologies that allow users to interact with digital worlds in fundamentally different ways. These technologies are often the most visible and immediate components of the Metaverse.

- **Virtual Reality (VR)**: VR immerses users in a completely digital environment. Using VR headsets, such as the **Oculus Rift** or **HTC Vive**, users are placed into 3D spaces where they can interact with the environment using hand controllers, motion tracking, and sometimes haptic feedback systems. VR allows users to experience fully immersive worlds, making it ideal for gaming, training, virtual meetings, and even remote exploration.
  - **Real-world Example**: *Meta's Horizon Workrooms* is a VR platform where users can meet, collaborate, and socialize in a virtual office environment. It allows people to create avatars, hold meetings in 3D spaces, share virtual whiteboards, and interact as though they were physically present together, even if they're in different locations around the world.
- **Augmented Reality (AR)**: Unlike VR, AR enhances the real world by overlaying digital elements (such as images, sounds, or data) on top

31

of the physical environment. AR is typically experienced through smartphones, tablets, or AR glasses like **Microsoft HoloLens** or **Google Glass**. AR allows for interactive experiences that bridge the digital and physical worlds, such as in navigation systems, entertainment, or education.

- o **Real-world Example**: *Pokémon Go* revolutionized mobile gaming by allowing players to interact with virtual Pokémon placed in real-world locations using their smartphones. The game used AR technology to blend the real world with digital content, allowing users to engage with their environment in a new and exciting way.

Both VR and AR are foundational to the Metaverse, as they enable users to step into and interact with virtual spaces or augment their physical surroundings with digital elements. Together, VR and AR create immersive experiences that are essential for the Metaverse's vision of interconnected virtual environments.

2. Blockchain Technology

Blockchain is a distributed ledger technology that securely stores data across multiple nodes in a decentralized way. In the context of the Metaverse, blockchain plays a crucial role in verifying ownership, enabling secure transactions, and fostering decentralized economies within virtual worlds. Blockchain allows users to own, trade, and sell digital assets such as virtual land, artwork, and items, which can be represented as **Non-Fungible Tokens (NFTs)**.

- **Real-world Example**: In **Decentraland**, a virtual world built on the Ethereum blockchain, users can purchase, sell, and trade virtual land and assets using the platform's native cryptocurrency, MANA. This decentralized approach gives users true ownership of their virtual assets, which can be traded on marketplaces. Blockchain ensures that the ownership of virtual land is secure, transparent, and immutable, creating a digital economy where users can monetize their creations and investments.

  o **NFTs in the Metaverse**: NFTs represent unique digital assets on the blockchain, and they have become an essential part of virtual worlds. In platforms like Decentraland, users can buy virtual clothing, art, and accessories as NFTs, ensuring that these items are one-of-a-kind and cannot be duplicated.

By using blockchain, the Metaverse introduces concepts of digital ownership, scarcity, and value to virtual worlds, enabling the creation of thriving economies and virtual marketplaces. Blockchain's transparency, security, and decentralization are key to ensuring trust within these environments.

3. Artificial Intelligence (AI)

Artificial Intelligence (AI) is used in the Metaverse to enhance user interactions, automate processes, and improve overall experiences. AI enables virtual worlds to have dynamic and responsive environments, from intelligent non-playable characters (NPCs) to adaptive game mechanics. In addition, AI is used to create personalized experiences for users, ensuring that the Metaverse feels alive and continuously evolving.

- **AI in NPCs and Virtual Assistants**: In virtual worlds, AI-powered NPCs can interact with users in realistic ways, providing information, guidance, or even acting as competitors or allies. AI can also be used to create personalized avatars that adapt to user preferences and behavior.
  - ○ **Real-world Example**: AI is used in platforms like **VRChat** to generate lifelike NPCs that respond to users with pre-programmed or dynamically generated responses, helping to enhance immersion. Similarly, AI can be employed in Metaverse games to create dynamic storylines where NPC behavior adapts based on the player's actions.
- **Personalization and Machine Learning**: Machine learning algorithms can analyze user data to personalize the virtual world experience, such as

adjusting difficulty levels in a game or recommending virtual goods and services based on past behavior. AI can also generate personalized content, such as virtual environments, tailored to a user's preferences.

AI will play an increasingly important role in shaping the Metaverse, ensuring that virtual environments are engaging, responsive, and personalized, making the experiences richer and more immersive.

4. Cloud Computing

Cloud Computing is the backbone of the Metaverse, providing the infrastructure needed to host virtual worlds, store large amounts of data, and support real-time interactions across the globe. Cloud computing allows developers to scale their virtual worlds to accommodate millions of users and ensures that data can be accessed from anywhere in the world.

- **Data Storage and Scalability**: Virtual worlds generate vast amounts of data, including user interactions, content creation, and assets. Cloud computing platforms, such as **Amazon Web Services (AWS)**, **Microsoft Azure**, and **Google Cloud**, provide the infrastructure to store and manage this data at scale. Cloud computing enables seamless updates to virtual

35

environments, ensures that users' data is securely stored, and allows for real-time processing of data.

- o **Real-world Example**: **Meta's Horizon Worlds** and other VR platforms rely on cloud computing to support their large-scale virtual environments. The cloud ensures that the virtual world remains persistent, meaning users can return to the same space or game without interruptions, and that virtual goods and assets are easily accessible no matter where users are located.
- **Streaming and Real-Time Interaction**: Cloud computing also enables real-time streaming and interaction in virtual worlds. Without the cloud, the amount of data required for multiplayer games or immersive VR experiences would be too large to handle locally. Cloud infrastructure ensures that virtual worlds are responsive and can handle the complexity of multiplayer interactions, making the Metaverse accessible to users across different devices.

The cloud allows virtual worlds to be scalable, always online, and responsive, enabling the global reach and persistent nature of the Metaverse.

Real-world Example: Integration of Blockchain, AI, and VR in the Metaverse

Let's consider how blockchain, AI, and VR come together in a modern Metaverse platform like **Decentraland** and **Meta's Horizon Workrooms**.

- **Decentraland**:

  Decentraland is a blockchain-based virtual world where users can buy virtual land, build digital properties, and trade assets. Blockchain allows for ownership and transactions of virtual land, ensuring transparency and security. AI helps power some of the interactions in Decentraland, like smart contracts and personalized avatars. Users can create and sell NFTs, which represent ownership of virtual goods and real estate. VR is also integrated, allowing users to experience the world in an immersive 3D environment. The combination of these technologies enables a decentralized virtual economy where ownership is verifiable, interactions are dynamic, and users can engage with the world in a lifelike manner.

- **Meta's Horizon Workrooms**:

  Horizon Workrooms is a virtual collaboration platform that integrates VR to allow users to interact in a 3D virtual office space. Users create avatars and engage in meetings, whiteboarding sessions, and brainstorming. The use of AI

37

helps in creating lifelike avatars that mimic real-world movements and speech. Additionally, cloud computing is used to host and manage these virtual spaces, ensuring that users can join meetings from anywhere in the world. Horizon Workrooms demonstrates how VR and AI can enhance social and professional interactions in the Metaverse, creating a space for collaboration, productivity, and innovation.

Conclusion

The Metaverse is built on a combination of powerful technologies, each contributing to the creation of immersive, interactive, and persistent virtual worlds. **VR** and **AR** provide the immersive experiences, **blockchain** enables decentralized ownership and virtual economies, **AI** drives personalization and interactive elements, and **cloud computing** ensures scalability and real-time interaction.

As the Metaverse continues to evolve, these technologies will converge to create even more sophisticated, engaging, and accessible virtual experiences. Understanding how these technologies work together is essential for developers, designers, and businesses looking to build or participate in the Metaverse, as they provide the foundation for everything from virtual goods and services to social interactions and real-time collaboration. The next chapter will explore how developers can use these technologies to build their own virtual worlds and applications in the Metaverse.

CHAPTER 4

PRINCIPLES OF VIRTUAL WORLD DESIGN

Overview: Discuss the Principles and Best Practices for Designing Immersive and Engaging Virtual Environments

Designing virtual worlds is a multifaceted process that blends creativity with technical precision. Whether you're creating a game, a social environment, or a virtual space for collaboration, the principles of virtual world design are crucial for ensuring that users have an immersive and engaging experience.

In this chapter, we'll explore the core principles of virtual world design, focusing on how to create environments that are not only functional but also enjoyable, interactive, and aesthetically pleasing. These principles are foundational to ensuring that users feel fully immersed in the world, whether they're exploring a fantastical landscape, collaborating in a virtual office, or playing a multiplayer game.

1. Immersion: Creating a Believable World

Immersion is one of the key elements of virtual world design. For a virtual world to be engaging, it must draw users in and make them feel as though they are part of that environment. The more immersive the experience, the more likely users are to stay engaged and return for repeated interactions.

- **Consistency**: The virtual world should have consistent rules, mechanics, and logic that allow users to understand how the world works and how they can interact with it. Whether it's a game or a social platform, ensuring that there is a clear structure and coherent design is crucial to avoid breaking immersion.

- **Visual Design**: The aesthetic appeal of a virtual world significantly affects the user's level of immersion. A visually stunning world with rich textures, lighting effects, and well-designed objects can enhance the experience, but it must align with the world's overall tone. A fantasy world might use soft, glowing lights and fantasy architecture, while a sci-fi setting might have sleek, metallic environments.

- **Audio Design**: Sound plays a huge role in immersing users in a virtual world. Ambient sounds, background music, and the sounds of interactions within the world (e.g., footsteps, birds chirping, or engine noises) all contribute to creating a more realistic and engaging environment. Realistic soundscapes help users feel like they truly belong in the space.

---

2. Interactivity: Designing for User Engagement

The best virtual worlds are not static—they are interactive. Interactivity allows users to influence their environment, whether by building, crafting, or solving challenges. It's this interaction that keeps users engaged and invested in the world.

- **User Control**: Giving users control over their avatars, surroundings, and environment fosters a deeper sense of ownership and engagement. Whether through customization options, movement freedom, or building systems, providing ways for users to personalize their experience is essential.

- **Responsive World**: The world itself must respond to user actions. A virtual world should have interactive objects, NPCs (Non-Player Characters), and systems that react to the user's presence or actions. For instance, a player's actions in a game may influence the storyline or affect their standing within the virtual economy.

- **Complexity and Rewards**: A good virtual world should strike a balance between simplicity and complexity. Too simple, and it will bore the user; too complex, and it will overwhelm them. Game mechanics like quests, challenges, and rewards create engagement and provide users with goals to work toward.

---

3. Social Dynamics: Fostering Connection and Collaboration

Social interaction is another crucial element in the design of virtual worlds, especially in the Metaverse, where shared experiences are central. Whether it's chatting with friends, collaborating on projects, or engaging in large-scale multiplayer events, the design should encourage socialization and collaboration.

- **Community Building**: Virtual worlds can be more than just a place to play or explore; they can be a place to build communities. Players can form groups, guilds, or teams to collaborate on tasks, create shared spaces, or compete against one another. Facilitating community building through social tools such as chat systems, forums, and group activities can lead to more engaging experiences.

- **Social Features**: Designing for communication is critical in creating a vibrant virtual community. Features like messaging, voice chat, and shared spaces where players can meet and interact (e.g., virtual lounges or meeting spaces) make the world feel more alive. Platforms like *VRChat* use avatars, voice interaction, and customizable spaces to create social interactions that feel natural and rewarding.

- **Multiplayer Integration**: Multiplayer interactions help create a more dynamic, evolving experience. Whether users are co-op gaming, competing against each other, or simply exploring together, allowing players to interact in meaningful ways can drive engagement.

4. User-Centered Design: Making the Experience Accessible

A good virtual world design must prioritize the user's experience, ensuring that the world is easy to navigate and interact with. From intuitive user interfaces to accessibility features, designing with the user in mind is paramount.

- **Usability**: The world should be easy to understand and navigate. From the moment a user logs in, the design should allow them to quickly grasp how to interact with the environment. This includes clear menus, in-game tutorials, and simple navigation systems.
- **Accessibility**: Accessibility is a critical consideration. A well-designed virtual world should be accessible to users with various abilities. This might include customizable controls, visual aids for those with vision impairments, or text-to-speech features for users with reading difficulties.

- **Intuitive Controls**: Especially in VR environments, controls should feel natural and intuitive. Whether it's using motion controllers to interact or hand gestures to navigate, the user should feel like they can manipulate the environment without frustration.

5. Scaling and Performance: Ensuring Smooth Experiences for All Users

As virtual worlds grow, scaling the experience to accommodate thousands (or even millions) of users becomes a challenge. Performance optimization ensures that the virtual environment remains responsive and enjoyable, even during high-traffic moments.

- **Optimizing Load Times**: Long loading times can break immersion and frustrate users. By designing virtual worlds that load quickly and maintain high performance, developers can ensure that users have a smooth experience when navigating different areas of the world.
- **Server Infrastructure**: Virtual worlds with large user bases need robust server infrastructure to handle multiplayer interactions and environmental updates in real time. Cloud-based solutions, edge computing, and distributed servers help ensure that performance is maintained as the world scales.

45

- **Balancing Detail with Performance**: While stunning visuals and intricate details are essential for immersion, they should not hinder the performance of the virtual world. Striking a balance between visual quality and smooth gameplay is crucial, especially in real-time interactions and multiplayer scenarios.

Real-world Example: Design Strategies Used in Popular Games like Fortnite and Minecraft

To better understand how these principles come together in a virtual world, let's look at how two highly successful games, *Fortnite* and *Minecraft*, incorporate design strategies that blend creativity with functionality.

Fortnite

Fortnite is a perfect example of how a well-designed virtual world can captivate millions of players. While it started as a battle royale game, *Fortnite* has evolved into a social hub where players can interact, engage in mini-games, and experience live events.

- **Immersive Design**: The game features a constantly changing environment, from seasonal updates to limited-time events that keep the world feeling dynamic and fresh.

The use of vibrant visuals, smooth animations, and well-designed soundscapes enhances the immersive experience.

- **Interactivity**: Players can interact with a wide range of objects, from weapons and vehicles to traps and structures. The building mechanic, where players can construct forts during gameplay, adds a layer of strategy and user-driven creativity to the game.

- **Social Interaction**: *Fortnite* has social features like voice chat, team-based play, and live events that bring players together. One of the most notable features is the **live in-game events**, such as virtual concerts or collaborative challenges, which allow players to interact with each other in unique ways.

- **Accessibility and Usability**: *Fortnite* has customizable controls for different platforms (PC, consoles, mobile) and supports cross-play, ensuring that players from various devices can engage together. The game also offers accessibility options like colorblind settings and subtitles.

Minecraft

Minecraft revolutionized the idea of creativity in virtual worlds, giving players the ability to shape and manipulate their environment to their heart's content. Its simple design hides a deep and complex system that allows for endless possibilities.

- **Immersive Design**: The blocky, pixelated graphics of *Minecraft* create a unique visual style that feels expansive and engaging. The world's procedurally generated landscapes provide a different experience each time the player starts a new game, offering endless exploration opportunities.

- **User-Centered Design**: The game allows for a variety of interaction types, from solo survival gameplay to cooperative building projects with friends. The interface is simple and intuitive, making it accessible to both young players and adults.

- **Social Collaboration**: *Minecraft* encourages collaboration, where players can build structures together, create their own mini-games, or explore each other's creations. The multiplayer mode supports large communities, allowing for massive user-generated worlds and projects.

- **Performance and Scalability**: Despite the simple graphics, *Minecraft* is optimized to run smoothly on a wide range of hardware. This scalability ensures that players on low-end devices can enjoy the game just as much as those with high-performance gaming rigs.

Conclusion

Designing a virtual world that is immersive, interactive, and engaging requires a thoughtful balance between creativity, technology, and user experience. The principles discussed in this chapter—immersion, interactivity, social dynamics, user-centered design, and performance—are key to creating virtual environments that users will want to explore and engage with for hours on end.

Games like *Fortnite* and *Minecraft* provide excellent examples of how these principles can be applied to create engaging, immersive, and successful virtual worlds. As the Metaverse continues to evolve, understanding and applying these design principles will be essential for developers looking to build the next generation of virtual experiences.

In the next chapter, we will explore how to take these design principles and apply them to real-world virtual world development, using the most popular tools and platforms available today.

CHAPTER 5

CREATING REALISTIC VIRTUAL ENVIRONMENTS

Overview: Techniques for Creating Immersive Virtual Spaces

Creating realistic virtual environments is at the core of crafting engaging and immersive experiences in the Metaverse. Whether you're developing a game, a virtual office, or an interactive tour, a virtual world is only as engaging as its ability to draw users in and make them feel like they are truly "there." To do this, designers rely on techniques in 3D modeling, texturing, lighting, and sound, among others.

In this chapter, we'll dive into the critical components involved in creating realistic virtual spaces. We'll explore how 3D modeling, textures, lighting, and sound all contribute to the feeling of presence in a virtual world. You'll learn how each of these elements can be optimized to create environments that are not only visually appealing but also highly interactive and immersive.

1. 3D Modeling: The Foundation of Virtual Worlds

3D modeling is the process of creating three-dimensional representations of objects or environments within a virtual space. It's the first step in bringing a virtual world to life, laying the groundwork for the environment's appearance and interactivity.

- **Polygonal   Modeling**: Most virtual environments rely on polygonal models, where 3D objects are made up of polygons—shapes with flat surfaces. Artists use 3D modeling software like **Blender**, **Maya**, or **3ds Max** to build models that represent everything from landscapes to furniture. The more polygons an object has, the higher its visual detail, but this comes at the cost of performance, so finding the right balance is key.

- **Procedural   Generation**: In many cases, designers use **procedural generation** techniques to create large, dynamic environments without having to manually model every asset. Procedural tools generate content based on algorithms and parameters, creating realistic environments such as mountains, forests, or cityscapes. Games like *No Man's Sky* use procedural generation to create vast, ever-expanding universes that players can explore.

- **Asset   Libraries**: Many virtual worlds use **asset libraries**, which are pre-built models that can be reused across various projects. These assets could include buildings, furniture, vehicles, and more. The use of asset libraries helps streamline the design process, allowing developers to focus on the more unique aspects of a virtual world while reusing common elements.

2. Textures: Adding Detail and Realism

Once the basic 3D models have been created, **textures** are applied to them to provide surface detail, such as colors, patterns, and finishes. Texturing is a vital part of virtual world design, as it gives objects a sense of realism and depth.

- **UV   Mapping**:
  UV mapping is the process of unwrapping a 3D model's surface so that a 2D texture can be applied to it. Think of it like peeling an orange and laying the peel flat. This process allows designers to apply detailed textures, like wood grain or stone, to a model in a way that wraps seamlessly around its surface.

- **Normal   and   Bump   Maps**:
  Normal maps and **bump maps** are used to add the illusion of depth to surfaces without actually increasing the model's polygon count. They simulate small details

like wrinkles, pores, or bumps on an object's surface, making it look more detailed than it really is.

- **PBR (Physically Based Rendering)**: **PBR** is a rendering technique that simulates how light interacts with surfaces in the real world. It helps create more realistic materials, such as metal, wood, or glass. PBR takes into account factors like roughness, reflectivity, and how light diffuses across surfaces, ensuring that textures look realistic under different lighting conditions.

- **Real-world Example**: Consider the application of textures in **VRTourViewer**, an immersive real estate viewing platform. In this case, the textures applied to interior walls, furniture, floors, and exteriors of homes must be high quality to ensure that users have a realistic and convincing experience while touring homes virtually. The textures used for materials like wood, marble, or concrete must feel natural and reflect light appropriately, so users feel as if they are really inside the property.

---

3. Lighting: Setting the Mood and Enhancing Realism

Lighting plays an essential role in how a virtual world looks and feels. The way light interacts with objects and surfaces can drastically affect the atmosphere and realism of the environment.

Effective lighting helps highlight key areas, create depth, and set the emotional tone of the space.

- **Types of Lighting**:
  - **Ambient Lighting**: Provides uniform illumination throughout the environment. It simulates natural light and ensures that there aren't any harsh shadows or overly dark areas.
  - **Point Lights**: These simulate light sources like bulbs or candles and shine outward in all directions, casting shadows and creating highlights.
  - **Directional Lights**: These simulate sunlight or other distant light sources and cast parallel rays of light.
  - **Spotlights**: A focused light that shines on a specific area, commonly used to highlight an object or draw attention to a particular detail.
- **Real-time vs. Baked Lighting**:
  - **Real-time Lighting**: Used in interactive virtual worlds where lighting needs to change dynamically. For example, in games, lighting must adjust to player movement, time of day, or weather.
  - **Baked Lighting**: Pre-computed lighting that doesn't change in real-time. This is often used for

static scenes or environments that don't require frequent updates.

- **Shadows and Reflections**: Realistic shadows and reflections add depth and realism to a virtual world. These effects are achieved using **ray tracing**, which simulates how light interacts with objects and surfaces. For instance, a shiny floor should reflect light and objects above it, while a lamp might cast a shadow on the walls around it.

- **Real-world Example**: In virtual real estate platforms like **VRTourViewer**, lighting is crucial for creating a lifelike experience. When users explore a property, they expect the lighting to mimic real-world conditions. Sunlight streaming through windows, shadows cast by furniture, and the way light changes as users move through a room all contribute to a convincing, immersive environment.

---

4. Sound Design: Bringing the Environment to Life

Sound is often an overlooked aspect of virtual world design, but it plays a major role in creating an immersive experience. Sound can convey a sense of presence, enhance the atmosphere, and provide important cues about the environment.

- **Ambient Sound**: Background sounds like wind, rain, traffic, or distant voices help establish the environment. For example, the sound of birds chirping in a park or the hum of machinery in an industrial area adds layers of realism to the virtual world.

- **Interactive Sounds**: Sounds tied to specific actions or events help guide users and enhance their interaction with the environment. For instance, a door opening or a chair creaking as a user sits can provide tactile feedback, even in a virtual space.

- **Spatial Audio**: Spatial or 3D audio gives users a sense of directionality. Sounds change depending on the user's location or orientation within the environment. For example, the sound of footsteps should get louder as the user approaches, and quieter as they walk away.

- **Real-world** **Example**: In **VRTourViewer**, the sound design for virtual property tours is vital in creating a realistic and immersive experience. The sound of footsteps on different surfaces (wood, carpet, tile), the ambient noise of wind through windows, or the hum of distant appliances all add to the authenticity of the environment. These sounds help users feel like they're actually walking through the property, even though they're exploring it remotely.

Conclusion

Creating realistic virtual environments is a complex, multi-layered process that involves combining a variety of design elements. **3D modeling**, **texturing**, **lighting**, and **sound** work together to create environments that feel believable and immersive. Whether you're designing a gaming world, a virtual office, or a real estate tour, mastering these elements is key to crafting an experience that users will find engaging and lifelike.

Real-world examples like the **VRTourViewer** platform demonstrate how these design principles can be used to create compelling virtual spaces, helping users interact with and experience digital environments in ways that mirror the physical world. As the Metaverse continues to grow and evolve, these techniques will play an integral role in shaping the future of virtual spaces.

In the next chapter, we will dive deeper into the process of creating **interactive systems and mechanics** that keep users engaged and help them navigate and influence their virtual environments.

CHAPTER 6

UNDERSTANDING SPATIAL DESIGN AND INTERACTION

Overview: How Users Interact with Objects and Spaces in Virtual Worlds, Including the Concept of Virtual Movement and Spatial Relationships

Designing effective spatial interactions in virtual worlds is a crucial aspect of creating an engaging and immersive experience. Unlike traditional forms of media, virtual worlds allow users to navigate, interact, and alter the environment in ways that feel intuitive and natural. Whether users are exploring an open-world game, participating in virtual meetings, or touring a museum, the way they move through and interact with spaces impacts their overall experience.

In this chapter, we'll examine how users engage with virtual environments, focusing on virtual movement, spatial relationships, and interaction systems that enhance immersion. From how objects are manipulated to how users move through 3D spaces, the principles of spatial design and interaction are essential to creating believable and enjoyable virtual worlds.

1. Virtual Movement: Navigating the Digital Landscape

Movement within a virtual world is an essential aspect of user interaction. Users need to feel in control as they navigate through spaces, whether it's walking, flying, or teleporting. Different systems allow for varying degrees of interaction and immersion, depending on the type of virtual world and the hardware being used.

- **First-Person and Third-Person Views**: In many virtual worlds, users can control an avatar in either a first-person or third-person view. In **first-person** perspective, users experience the environment as though they are seeing through the eyes of their avatar, which is ideal for immersion in games or VR experiences. In **third-person** perspective, the user controls the avatar from an external viewpoint, which is more common in platformers and RPGs.

- **Locomotion in VR**: Virtual reality (VR) adds an extra layer of interaction, as users are able to move physically within the environment. VR uses either **room-scale movement**, where users can walk around within a limited area, or **teleportation-based movement**, where users point to a location and "teleport" to it. VR locomotion is a delicate balance, as it must feel natural without inducing discomfort, such as **motion sickness**.

- **Real-world** **Example**:
  In *Half-Life: Alyx*, users navigate through an immersive 3D world using both hand controllers and head movements. The game employs a natural locomotion system where users can walk, crouch, or jump, depending on the environment. The VR system also integrates teleportation, so users can quickly move to areas they've already explored without moving in real time. This balance of movement methods helps enhance the immersive experience while avoiding discomfort, a common challenge in VR.

- **Non-VR** **Movement**:
  In games and virtual spaces not designed for VR, users typically navigate through **keyboard and mouse controls** or **gamepads**. These systems simulate movement through digital environments and rely heavily on intuitive controls for direction and speed.

---

2. Spatial Relationships: Understanding How Objects Relate to Each Other

Spatial relationships within virtual worlds define how objects are placed and how users interact with them. A key part of designing virtual worlds is ensuring that these relationships feel realistic and allow users to interact naturally with their surroundings.

- **Proximity and Interaction Zones**: One key principle of spatial design is defining **interaction zones**. These are virtual areas where objects or characters respond to user actions. For example, objects within a specific range might become interactable when the user approaches them, such as opening a door or picking up an item.

- **Object Manipulation**: Allowing users to manipulate objects within a virtual world (e.g., picking up, rotating, or moving items) creates a sense of agency. In VR, this is especially important, as users physically engage with objects through hand controllers. The mechanics of these interactions—such as the weight of an object, its texture, and how it responds to the user—play a significant role in creating a realistic sense of presence.

- **Real-world Example**: In *Half-Life: Alyx*, users can interact with a variety of objects, including opening drawers, grabbing guns, or solving puzzles. The interaction system is designed to mimic real-world behavior, such as physically pulling a lever or pushing a button. This spatial interaction not only allows users to engage with the environment but also creates a more immersive experience by allowing them to interact with the world in a physically intuitive way.

- **Perspective and Depth**: Another important element of spatial design is the use of **depth perception**. In virtual worlds, designers use various techniques such as lighting, object scaling, and perspective to simulate a sense of distance. These cues help users understand where they are in space, where they can go, and how far objects are.

3. Interaction Systems: Enhancing Engagement through Responsive Environments

Interaction systems are the mechanisms by which users interact with objects and other users in a virtual world. These systems vary depending on the platform (e.g., VR, desktop, mobile) and the goals of the virtual space, whether it's a game, a simulation, or a social environment.

- **User-Driven Interaction**: User-driven interaction refers to the ability for the player or user to actively shape the world around them. In games like *Minecraft*, players can build, modify, and destroy blocks to shape the world. Similarly, in virtual worlds like **Second Life**, users have complete control over the creation and modification of their avatars, spaces, and objects.

- **Contextual** **Interaction**:
  Many virtual environments use contextual interaction systems where certain actions are available only under specific conditions. For example, in a game, players might only be able to interact with certain objects when they meet specific requirements or reach a certain level. Similarly, in social platforms like **VRChat**, users can interact with objects and spaces based on their role in the environment (e.g., as a creator, visitor, or moderator).

- **Multi-User** **Interaction**:
  In shared virtual spaces, interaction is not just limited to objects, but also to other users. Multi-user interaction is a cornerstone of many virtual worlds, allowing players to collaborate, socialize, or compete. Effective interaction systems ensure that users can communicate (via text, voice, or gestures), cooperate (e.g., completing challenges together), and build relationships within the virtual world.

- **Real-world** **Example**:
  In virtual museum tours like the **Louvre VR Tour**, interaction systems allow users to explore artifacts, read descriptions, and engage with information in different ways. Users can select pieces of art to view up close, zoom in for detailed inspection, and even listen to explanations from virtual guides. The interactive systems in these virtual tours are designed to replicate the experience of being in the museum while providing

additional tools for engagement, such as audio and visual aids.

---

4. Designing Immersive Experiences: Balancing Realism with Gameplay

While realistic interactions are crucial to creating an engaging virtual world, it's also important to balance realism with fun and accessibility. Not all interactions need to be completely realistic; sometimes, the experience is better when it is exaggerated, simplified, or gamified.

- **Game   Mechanics**:
  In many virtual worlds, designers incorporate gameplay mechanics that enhance interaction. For example, in a virtual world, players might encounter puzzles or challenges that require them to use the environment or objects in creative ways. These mechanics encourage users to interact with the world more deeply, ensuring that the experience is both entertaining and engaging.

- **Immersion   vs.   Functionality**:
  While realism is important, certain virtual environments prioritize **functional interaction** over **real-world accuracy**. For instance, teleportation in VR environments is often used to help users move between large spaces without requiring real physical movement, which might

cause discomfort. This form of interaction is designed to make the experience more comfortable, rather than strictly adhering to real-world rules of physics.

- **User Feedback and Interaction Quality**: To enhance immersion, interaction systems should provide feedback. This can include haptic feedback when users interact with objects, visual cues like glowing outlines around interactive objects, or auditory signals that reinforce the action. Feedback reassures the user that their actions are having an effect on the environment, helping to maintain immersion.

Real-world Example: Interaction Systems in Half-Life: Alyx and the Louvre VR Tour

- **Half-Life: Alyx**: *Half-Life: Alyx* is one of the most sophisticated examples of virtual interaction and spatial design in VR. The game features highly interactive environments where users can physically manipulate objects using hand controllers. For example, players can open drawers, search for hidden items, and even throw objects. The environment reacts to their actions in real-time, and the spatial relationships between objects (such as the distance and weight of items) make the interactions feel natural and immersive. The design of movement systems, such as teleportation or walking in VR, ensures that players feel both in control and comfortable, reducing potential motion sickness while maintaining immersion.

- **Louvre VR Tour**: The **Louvre VR Tour** offers a great example of spatial interaction in a non-gaming environment. Users can explore the famous museum's exhibits virtually, navigating through rooms, zooming in on artworks, and interacting with objects for a closer look. The interaction systems are simple but effective: clicking on an artifact to view more details or listening to narrated information about an exhibit. The virtual space feels expansive, and the interaction systems replicate a real-world museum experience while adding elements that digital environments enable, such as the ability to teleport between different rooms or zoom in on intricate details.

Conclusion

Understanding spatial design and interaction is essential for creating virtual worlds that are not only functional but also immersive and engaging. By focusing on how users move through environments, interact with objects, and engage with other users, developers can design virtual worlds that feel real and responsive.

As demonstrated by *Half-Life: Alyx* and the *Louvre VR Tour*, interaction systems can greatly enhance the user experience by offering intuitive and immersive ways to navigate and engage with virtual spaces. By mastering these principles of spatial design and interaction, developers can build virtual worlds that provide users with rich, engaging experiences that keep them coming back for more.

In the next chapter, we will explore how to design and implement **interactive systems** that respond to user actions, further enhancing the overall experience and engagement within virtual worlds.

CHAPTER 7

DESIGNING FOR IMMERSION: AUDIO AND VISUALS

Overview: How Sound Design and Visual Aesthetics Enhance User Immersion, Including the Importance of Haptic Feedback and Sensory Design

One of the most powerful elements of creating an immersive virtual world is the ability to engage multiple senses at once. While visual and auditory design are often the first considerations in building immersive virtual environments, incorporating haptic feedback and sensory cues into the experience is just as important. These elements work together to create a cohesive, engaging environment where users feel as though they are physically present in the virtual world.

In this chapter, we'll explore the crucial role of **audio design**, **visual aesthetics**, and **haptic feedback** in enhancing immersion. We'll also discuss how sensory design is used to evoke emotional responses, improve interaction, and ensure users feel deeply connected to the virtual space.

1. Visual Design: Crafting the World You See

Visual aesthetics form the first layer of immersion in a virtual environment. The way a world looks—its textures, lighting, models, and overall art direction—sets the tone and atmosphere, guiding the user's experience and emotional response.

- **Realism vs. Stylization**: When designing for immersion, a key consideration is whether to pursue realism or a more stylized approach. Realistic environments, with their high-quality textures and lighting, can make users feel as though they are truly inside a space. On the other hand, stylized worlds, like those in *Fortnite* or *Minecraft*, often prioritize creative expression, yet they still maintain a sense of immersion through consistent design and color palettes.

- **Lighting and Shadows**: Lighting plays a major role in shaping the mood and realism of a virtual environment. Proper use of light can emphasize key elements, guide users, and create atmosphere. Shadows, reflections, and dynamic lighting (such as day-night cycles) all contribute to the visual complexity and immersion of the world.

- **Depth and Perspective**: Depth is an essential component of visual design, and it is achieved through techniques such as **parallax scrolling**, where background and foreground elements move at different speeds to create a sense of distance. Additionally, **field of view (FOV)** and **perspective distortion** can be adjusted to simulate real-world vision, helping to make virtual spaces feel more natural.

- **Visual Cues for Interaction**: A well-designed virtual world uses visual cues to tell the user what can and cannot be interacted with. This could include highlighting objects that can be manipulated, changing their appearance when the user is nearby, or adding animations to show an object is interactive.

---

2. Audio Design: The Sound of Immersion

Sound design plays an equally important role in enhancing immersion. It helps to establish the atmosphere of the environment, guide the user's actions, and provide real-time feedback. Sound design for virtual worlds can include environmental sounds, effects, voiceovers, and interactive audio cues.

- **Ambient Soundscapes**: Ambient sound is the background noise that helps set the tone of the environment. Whether it's the gentle hum of a futuristic city, the chirping of birds in a forest, or the rustle of leaves in the wind, these sounds contribute to the world's authenticity and guide the user's emotional state.

- **Interactive   Sounds**:
Interactive sounds provide feedback to users when they take action within the virtual environment. For instance, the sound of footsteps walking on different surfaces, the swoosh of a door opening, or the ding of a button press all let users know they've interacted with an object or taken an action.

- **Spatial   Audio**:
One of the most important aspects of immersive audio in virtual worlds is **spatial audio**, where sounds are positioned in 3D space relative to the user's location. In spatial audio systems, the direction and distance of sounds change based on the user's movement and orientation, creating a sense of presence and depth.

  - **Real-world Example**: In **VRChat**, spatial audio is used extensively to simulate real-world experiences. When users speak, the sound of their voice is heard based on their virtual position in the environment. If a user moves closer, their voice becomes louder, and as they walk away, it fades. This creates an intuitive and natural sense of social interaction that mirrors real-world communication.

- **Sound   Cues   for   Navigation**:
Sounds can also be used to guide users through a virtual world. For example, when navigating a large open world,

subtle sound cues can signal nearby interactive objects or lead users to important areas. In a game, sound cues can be used to direct the player's attention to a new objective or trigger an event.

3. Haptic Feedback: The Sense of Touch in Virtual Worlds

Haptic feedback is an essential component of immersion, especially in virtual reality. It refers to the use of touch sensations to simulate physical interaction with virtual objects. By providing feedback through vibrations or forces, haptic devices enhance the user's sense of realism and make interactions feel more tangible.

- **VR Controllers and Haptic Feedback**: In VR, controllers like the **Oculus Touch** or **HTC Vive** wands are equipped with haptic motors that simulate sensations of touch, resistance, or impact. When users interact with virtual objects, the controllers provide feedback that mimics the weight, texture, or action of the object being manipulated.

- **Real-world   Example**: In *Beat Saber*, a popular rhythm-based VR game, players use VR controllers to slice through blocks to the beat of the music. The controllers vibrate in response to the player's actions, providing feedback when they hit a block, adding a physical element to the gameplay experience. This tactile sensation makes the user feel more immersed in the world, creating a deeper sense of connection to the game.

- **Enhanced Interactions**: Haptic feedback can be used to simulate physical sensations such as the feeling of a weapon recoil, the tension of a rope, or the texture of a surface. These small tactile cues make virtual interactions feel more realistic and rewarding. In action games or VR simulations, haptic feedback can even be used to simulate the sensation of walking, running, or jumping in the virtual world.

4. Sensory Design: Combining Audio, Visual, and Haptic Feedback

Immersion in the Metaverse is not limited to one sense alone—it's the combination of **audio**, **visuals**, and **haptics** that creates a truly immersive experience. When these sensory elements are designed to complement each other, users feel more connected to the virtual world.

- **Synergy Between Audio and Visuals**: In immersive environments, the visual and auditory elements should work together. For example, if a player sees an explosion or fire in a virtual environment, they should hear the corresponding sound effect of the explosion and feel the heat or impact through haptic feedback. When these elements are synchronized, the sense of immersion is strengthened.

- **Emotional Impact**: Sound and visual design are also crucial in evoking emotional responses from users. Dark, ambient soundscapes with eerie visuals can create tension and fear, while bright colors and cheerful music can foster a sense of joy and exploration. The goal is to design these sensory cues to influence how the user feels in different parts of the virtual world.

- **Real-world Example**: The immersive experience in *Beat Saber* is a perfect example of combining visuals, audio, and haptics. The intense music, the flashing blocks that react to the rhythm, and the haptic feedback from the controllers all work together to create an experience that is exhilarating and fully engaging. The design of the game encourages users to physically move in sync with the music, amplifying the sensory engagement.

- **Consistency in Sensory Design**: For immersion to be truly effective, sensory elements must be consistent across the entire virtual environment. Inconsistencies, such as disjointed sound or odd visual effects, can break immersion and distract users. Ensuring that all sensory elements match the world's tone and aesthetic is essential for maintaining engagement.

Real-world Example: The Sound Design in VR Experiences like Beat Saber and VRChat

- **Beat   Saber**:
  In *Beat Saber*, the sound design plays a central role in the immersion of the experience. The rhythmic beats, combined with the visual effects of the glowing blocks and the haptic feedback from the controllers, create a high-energy experience. The sound cues in the game are designed to guide players through the gameplay, providing a rhythmic pulse that aligns with the actions the player needs to take. The haptic feedback from the controllers, such as the slight vibrations when slicing through blocks, enhances the physicality of the game and helps users feel more connected to the experience.

- **VRChat**:
  VRChat takes immersion to the next level by integrating spatial audio into its social experience. In this virtual world, users' voices are not only heard based on their actions but also by their position in the virtual environment. If users are standing close to one another, their voices sound louder, and as they move away, their voices fade. This spatial design creates a natural, social interaction experience and makes the virtual world feel

more alive. Combined with the customizable avatars and real-time interaction, the sound design in *VRChat* enhances the sense of presence, making it feel as though users are truly sharing space in a virtual world.

Conclusion

Designing for immersion involves much more than just creating visually stunning environments. By integrating **sound design**, **visual aesthetics**, and **haptic feedback**, developers can create virtual worlds that engage all of the user's senses, heightening the feeling of presence and making the experience more memorable.

As demonstrated in *Beat Saber* and *VRChat*, the combination of immersive visuals, dynamic sound, and interactive feedback is essential for creating truly engaging virtual experiences. In the next chapter, we will explore how **interactive systems and mechanics** further enhance immersion by allowing users to engage with the world and affect change within it.

CHAPTER 8

USER AVATARS AND CUSTOMIZATION

Overview: The Importance of Avatars in User Representation, Customization Options, and Digital Identity

In virtual worlds, avatars are more than just digital representations—they are an extension of the user's identity. Whether in video games, social platforms, or virtual workspaces, avatars serve as the primary method of interacting with others and navigating through digital spaces. The ability to create and customize an avatar is one of the most important features in virtual world design because it allows users to express themselves, build a digital identity, and connect with others in meaningful ways.

This chapter explores the importance of avatars in virtual environments, focusing on the role they play in user representation, identity, and personalization. We will also dive into the customization options available to users, looking at how these elements affect user experience and engagement. Additionally, we will examine real-world examples from popular platforms like **Roblox** and immersive virtual worlds like those in *Ready Player One*, highlighting the potential of avatars to enhance social interaction and user engagement.

1. The Role of Avatars in User Representation

Avatars serve as a user's representation within a virtual world. They allow individuals to interact with others, explore environments, and participate in activities while reflecting their personal preferences and identity.

- **Personal   Expression**:
  Avatars are a form of self-expression, enabling users to reflect their personal style, interests, or alter ego within the digital realm. Whether users choose to represent themselves in a highly realistic way or opt for a fantastical character (like an animal or superhero), avatars offer a canvas for creative expression.

- **Digital   Identity**:
  An avatar often becomes a user's digital identity—a persona that represents them in virtual worlds. Just as people curate their online presence in social media, avatars are the visual manifestation of how users wish to present themselves in a virtual environment. This is especially important in virtual communities, where identity and social connections are central to the experience.

- **Community   and   Social   Interactions**:
  In social VR platforms or multiplayer games, avatars are essential for social interaction. They help users connect

with others, form friendships, and collaborate on tasks. Having a recognizable, personalized avatar makes it easier for others to identify users, fostering a sense of community.

- **Real-world** **Example**: In *VRChat*, an immensely popular virtual social platform, avatars are the focal point of the user experience. Users can create or choose from a wide range of avatars—anything from simple human representations to fantastical creatures or objects. The avatar becomes the primary method of communication and connection, with social interactions revolving around how users perceive and interact with each other's avatars.

---

2. The Importance of Avatar Customization

Customization is one of the most appealing aspects of virtual worlds. The ability to modify avatars—changing their appearance, clothing, accessories, and more—empowers users to design a version of themselves that aligns with their personal style or imagination. Customization adds depth and individuality to the virtual experience, allowing users to stand out, express their personality, and engage with the world in a unique way.

- **Appearance** **Customization**: Most platforms offer a range of options for customizing the basic features of avatars, such as skin color, body type, height, facial features, and more. This flexibility allows users to create avatars that mirror their real-world selves, or they can go in an entirely different direction by designing fantastical or abstract representations.

- **Clothing and Accessories**: In many virtual worlds, avatars can wear a variety of outfits, from casual clothing to elaborate costumes or accessories. These customizations help users reflect their identity or role within the world, such as a casual gamer, a business professional, or a medieval knight. Many platforms even allow users to purchase or trade in-game fashion, creating an in-world economy based on virtual goods.

- **Functional Customization**: Beyond aesthetics, customization can also serve functional purposes. In multiplayer games, users may customize avatars for specific roles or abilities. For example, in role-playing games (RPGs), players might choose an avatar's equipment, skills, and abilities based on the role they want to play within the group.

- **Real-world Example**: **Roblox**, one of the most popular online gaming platforms, provides users with a vast range of avatar customization options. Players can select from different body types, clothing items, accessories, and animations to create an avatar that is uniquely their own. Roblox also allows for user-generated content, where players can design and sell their own outfits, hair, and accessories, contributing to the platform's thriving economy. This customization plays a key role in user engagement, as players not only create avatars for themselves but also build and trade items for others.

---

3. The Impact of Avatar Customization on User Engagement

The ability to customize avatars impacts the level of engagement a user has with a virtual world. A more personalized avatar can lead to stronger emotional connections, greater investment in the virtual environment, and longer playtimes.

- **Identity and Connection**: Customization helps users form a deeper connection to their avatar, which in turn fosters emotional investment in the virtual world. When users can create an avatar that represents them—whether it's a digital reflection of their real-world self or a fantasy character—they feel more immersed in the experience and more likely to return to the platform regularly.
- **Self-Expression and Social Interaction**: In virtual worlds, socialization is often driven by avatar appearance. Users can express themselves through their

avatars, sharing aspects of their identity or creativity with others. This makes social interactions more meaningful, as people can connect with each other not just through text or voice, but through visual representation.

- **Incentivizing   Engagement**: Many virtual worlds offer incentives for users to customize their avatars. These incentives could include achievements, special items, or rewards for completing in-game challenges or participating in events. This further drives engagement, as users are motivated to personalize and improve their avatars as part of their in-game experience.

4. Digital Identity in the Metaverse

As the Metaverse grows and evolves, the role of avatars in defining and maintaining digital identity becomes even more significant. In virtual worlds, users have the opportunity to create a version of themselves that transcends the physical limitations of the real world.

- **Cross-Platform   Avatars**: One of the emerging trends in the Metaverse is the ability for users to carry their avatars across different virtual worlds. Platforms like **Decentraland** and **The Sandbox** are exploring ways to create interoperable avatars that can be used across multiple environments, creating a unified digital identity for users as they move between worlds. This opens up new possibilities for how users present themselves and interact with others in different virtual spaces.

- **NFTs and Ownership**: With the rise of blockchain technology and NFTs (Non-Fungible Tokens), users can now own digital avatars, items, and assets in a way that was not possible before. These avatars can be bought, sold, or traded, giving users true ownership of their digital identity. In virtual worlds such as **Decentraland**, users can purchase and modify avatars that are represented as NFTs, ensuring that their avatar is unique and verifiable.

- **Real-world Example**: In the movie *Ready Player One*, the concept of an avatar is central to the narrative. The main character, Wade Watts, uses his avatar in the OASIS, a fully immersive virtual world, to represent himself and interact with others. The avatars in *Ready Player One* can be highly customized, allowing users to create an identity that is a blend of their real-world persona and their idealized digital self. The avatars in the movie reflect the importance of digital identity in the Metaverse and how users can shape and present themselves in virtual spaces.

Conclusion

User avatars and customization play a critical role in defining personal identity and engagement within virtual worlds. Avatars are not only a way to represent oneself visually but also serve as a means of self-expression, social connection, and interaction. The ability to customize these avatars—whether through physical appearance, clothing, or accessories—adds depth to the user experience, creating a sense of ownership and investment in the virtual world.

Platforms like **Roblox** and the Metaverse-inspired world in *Ready Player One* illustrate the significance of avatar customization and digital identity in creating vibrant, engaging virtual spaces. As the Metaverse continues to evolve, the role of avatars will only become more integral, influencing how users interact with each other, express themselves, and create lasting connections in digital spaces.

In the next chapter, we will explore **designing interactive systems and mechanics** that allow users to engage with these avatars and virtual worlds in meaningful ways, further enhancing the immersion and user experience.

CHAPTER 9

INTRODUCTION TO METAVERSE DEVELOPMENT TOOLS

Overview: Overview of Key Development Platforms and Tools Used to Build Virtual Worlds, Including Unity, Unreal Engine, and WebXR

As the Metaverse grows and evolves, developing virtual worlds and experiences that are immersive, engaging, and accessible requires powerful tools and platforms. The development of virtual worlds is a complex task, often involving a mix of design, programming, and real-time interaction. Fortunately, there are several development tools available that enable creators to bring their ideas to life, from full-scale 3D games to virtual reality (VR) spaces and browser-based environments.

In this chapter, we will provide an overview of the key development platforms and tools used in building virtual worlds, with a focus on widely-used engines and technologies such as **Unity**, **Unreal Engine**, and **WebXR**. We'll also explore how these tools are utilized in popular platforms like **VRChat** and **Roblox**, showcasing real-world applications of virtual world development.

1. Unity: The Workhorse of Virtual World Development

Unity is one of the most widely used game engines for creating virtual environments. Known for its flexibility, cross-platform compatibility, and ease of use, Unity is favored by both indie developers and large studios alike. It's a powerful tool for building 2D and 3D games, virtual reality experiences, simulations, and more. Unity supports a wide range of platforms, from desktop and mobile devices to consoles, VR/AR headsets, and even the web.

- **Core Features of Unity**:
    - o **Cross-Platform Development**: Unity allows developers to create virtual worlds that run across multiple platforms, including Windows, macOS, PlayStation, Xbox, mobile devices, and VR/AR platforms like Oculus Rift and HTC Vive.
    - o **3D Modeling and Asset Integration**: Unity provides tools for creating 3D models, animations, and assets, or importing assets from other software. This makes it easy to build and populate virtual worlds with complex environments and interactive objects.
    - o **Real-time Rendering**: Unity's real-time rendering engine allows for the efficient creation of interactive and dynamic virtual environments.

Developers can see changes immediately, making it ideal for iterative design and rapid prototyping.

- o **Physics and Collision Detection**: Unity's built-in physics engine helps simulate real-world interactions within virtual worlds, such as gravity, object movement, and collision detection.
- o **Scripting and Interaction**: Using **C#** scripting, developers can program interactions, behaviors, and game mechanics in virtual environments. Unity's versatility makes it easy to integrate complex AI, interactive systems, and user inputs.

- **Real-world** **Example**: *VRChat* is a social VR platform that allows users to interact with others in a variety of virtual worlds. These worlds are created using Unity, allowing developers to design fully immersive spaces with customizable avatars, interactive objects, and multi-user support. In *VRChat*, users can explore user-generated content, play games, attend virtual events, and socialize in real-time. Unity's ability to handle 3D assets, dynamic lighting, and real-time interactions makes it an ideal tool for creating these engaging virtual spaces.

2. Unreal Engine: Advanced Graphics and High-Performance Worlds

Unreal Engine (UE) is another powerful game engine that has been used to create some of the most graphically intense and immersive virtual worlds. While both Unity and Unreal are highly capable engines, Unreal Engine shines when it comes to high-quality graphics and advanced rendering capabilities. It's often used in larger, more resource-intensive virtual worlds, games, and simulations, offering cutting-edge tools for developers looking to create stunning visuals.

- **Core Features of Unreal Engine**:
  - **High-Quality Graphics and Rendering**: Unreal Engine uses the **Unreal Engine 5** features such as **Nanite** and **Lumen** for high-fidelity graphics and lighting, making it an ideal tool for creating photorealistic environments and complex 3D models.
  - **Blueprint Visual Scripting**: Unreal Engine's **Blueprint** system allows developers to create game mechanics and interactions without writing code. This system provides a more intuitive way to design game logic, animations, and interactions, which is particularly beneficial for non-programmers.

- o **VR/AR Support**: Unreal Engine fully supports VR and AR development. It's widely used to create virtual worlds and immersive experiences for platforms like Oculus, HTC Vive, and PlayStation VR. The engine is known for handling complex VR worlds with high frame rates, which is critical to ensuring a smooth and comfortable experience for users.

- o **Advanced Physics and AI**: Unreal Engine provides robust tools for simulating realistic physics and behaviors. Whether it's object movement, collision detection, or AI-powered characters, UE can create dynamic, interactive environments that respond naturally to user input.

- **Real-world** **Example**: Unreal Engine has been used in the development of **high-quality virtual worlds** in both gaming and non-gaming sectors. One notable example is the use of Unreal Engine to create **highly detailed, interactive worlds** in the **Oculus**-based VR experiences. Unreal Engine's cutting-edge graphics capabilities are perfect for developers looking to create photorealistic environments that require high levels of performance, such as virtual art galleries or 3D architectural visualizations.

3. WebXR: Bringing Virtual Worlds to the Browser

WebXR is an API that allows developers to create virtual and augmented reality experiences that run directly in web browsers. WebXR is designed to work across different devices, from desktop computers and smartphones to VR and AR headsets, providing a universal platform for building accessible virtual worlds. Unlike traditional game engines like Unity or Unreal, WebXR is primarily focused on delivering virtual experiences through web browsers without requiring any additional software installations.

- **Core Features of WebXR:**
  - **Cross-Device Compatibility**: WebXR is designed to work across a variety of devices, including VR headsets, AR glasses, smartphones, and desktop computers. This makes it an ideal platform for creating virtual worlds that are easily accessible and don't require users to install heavy applications or software.
  - **Easy Access via the Web**: Because WebXR is built on web standards (HTML, JavaScript, and WebGL), users can access virtual worlds directly from their browser, without the need for specialized hardware or applications. This lowers the barrier to entry and makes virtual spaces more accessible to a wider audience.

- o **Lightweight Virtual Worlds**: WebXR is typically used for lighter, less resource-intensive virtual environments. While it may not offer the same level of complexity and high-performance rendering as Unity or Unreal Engine, it excels at creating simple, interactive virtual worlds that can run efficiently on various devices.

- o **AR and VR Integration**: WebXR allows developers to create both AR and VR experiences. Whether it's an immersive VR gallery or a simple AR app that overlays information on the real world, WebXR supports the creation of both types of experiences.

- **Real-world   Example**: **Roblox**, a popular gaming platform, also supports virtual world creation that runs directly in a web browser, similar to WebXR experiences. Although Roblox primarily relies on its own proprietary game engine, WebXR offers a similar functionality for creating interactive experiences within the browser. In the case of platforms like **VRChat**, where user-generated content and worlds are uploaded and shared, WebXR plays a role in enabling easy access to virtual experiences directly through a web interface, making the Metaverse more accessible for users without high-performance hardware.

4. Other Tools for Metaverse Development

In addition to Unity, Unreal Engine, and WebXR, there are a variety of other tools and technologies that contribute to the development of virtual worlds. These tools address different aspects of development, from 3D modeling and animation to scripting and interaction design.

- **Blender**: A powerful open-source tool for 3D modeling and animation. Blender is used extensively by developers to create models, environments, and animations for virtual worlds.
- **Maya and 3ds Max**: Industry-standard tools for creating detailed 3D models, characters, and animations. These tools are commonly used in high-end game and virtual world development.
- **Substance Painter**: A popular tool for texturing 3D models, allowing developers to create realistic materials and textures for virtual objects and environments.
- **Node.js**: Used for creating backend services that support multiplayer interaction, in-game economies, and user-generated content in virtual worlds.

Real-world Example: Building Virtual Worlds in Unity for Platforms Like VRChat and Roblox

- **VRChat**:

  VRChat is one of the most well-known social VR platforms, and much of its content is created using Unity. Developers use Unity to design interactive worlds and avatars that users can explore and customize. The Unity engine allows VRChat developers to create complex, interactive environments and optimize them for performance on VR hardware like the Oculus Rift and HTC Vive. In VRChat, users can teleport between different worlds, engage with NPCs, or participate in social activities—all powered by Unity's robust tools for 3D modeling, interaction, and animation.

- **Roblox**:

  Roblox is a user-generated platform that enables creators to build and share their virtual worlds. Roblox uses its own engine, but the basic principles of virtual world development (such as asset creation, scripting, and user interaction) are similar to those in Unity. Developers use Roblox Studio, a tool based on Unity, to create games, environments, and interactive content for millions of users worldwide. The platform supports cross-platform play, and users can customize their avatars, build new worlds, and engage with the content created by others.

Conclusion

Developing virtual worlds for the Metaverse requires a diverse toolkit of platforms and technologies. **Unity**, **Unreal Engine**, and **WebXR** provide the essential frameworks for creating everything from immersive VR environments to browser-based experiences. These tools, along with other software for modeling, animation, and scripting, give developers the power to build interactive, engaging virtual worlds that cater to a wide range of user needs.

As demonstrated by **VRChat** and **Roblox**, the tools you choose for developing virtual worlds shape both the experience you can offer users and the level of engagement possible within the virtual environment. In the next chapter, we will explore **designing interactive systems** within these virtual worlds, enabling users to interact with and affect their surroundings in meaningful ways.

CHAPTER 10

GAME ENGINES FOR THE METAVERSE

Overview: In-Depth Look at Using Game Engines like Unity and Unreal Engine to Create 3D Worlds for the Metaverse

Game engines are the backbone of most virtual worlds, including those in the Metaverse. These powerful tools allow developers to create 3D environments, interactive systems, and immersive experiences that users can explore and interact with. Unity and Unreal Engine are two of the most widely used game engines in the Metaverse space, offering comprehensive features and tools for designing everything from simple virtual spaces to complex, high-fidelity worlds.

In this chapter, we will take an in-depth look at how **Unity** and **Unreal Engine** are utilized to build 3D worlds for the Metaverse. We will also discuss how these game engines integrate with VR platforms, multiplayer systems, and other key features essential for Metaverse development. Additionally, we will highlight real-world examples of how these game engines are applied in popular Metaverse-related experiences.

1. Unity: A Versatile Game Engine for the Metaverse

Unity is one of the most widely used game engines for creating 3D environments and experiences, especially in the Metaverse. Its flexibility, ease of use, and robust feature set make it ideal for creating virtual worlds, simulations, games, and interactive experiences. Unity is particularly known for its ability to support a wide variety of platforms, including desktop, mobile, VR, AR, and even web browsers.

- **Core Features of Unity for Metaverse Development**:
    - **Cross-Platform Compatibility**: Unity allows developers to create content that can be deployed across multiple platforms, such as PCs, consoles, mobile devices, and VR/AR headsets like **Oculus Rift** or **HTC Vive**. This makes Unity a great choice for developers looking to create virtual experiences that can reach users on various devices.
    - **Asset Store**: Unity's Asset Store provides a wide range of pre-built assets, including 3D models, textures, animations, and scripts. This helps speed up development by allowing developers to use ready-made assets and focus on customizing and enhancing the world.
    - **Real-Time Rendering**: Unity uses a powerful real-time rendering engine that allows developers

to see changes instantly. This is essential for rapid prototyping and testing, particularly in dynamic, interactive environments.

o **VR/AR Integration**: Unity provides full support for VR and AR development, enabling developers to create immersive experiences for headsets like **Oculus**, **HTC Vive**, and **PlayStation VR**. It offers tools for motion tracking, hand gestures, and interactions that are crucial for VR development.

o **Scripting with C#**: Unity uses **C#** as its primary scripting language, making it accessible to developers familiar with object-oriented programming. With C#, developers can create complex game mechanics, interactive systems, and behaviors within their virtual worlds.

- **Real-world   Example**: One of Unity's most notable real-world applications in the Metaverse is its **integration with Oculus for VR game development**. Oculus is one of the leading VR platforms, and Unity has been integral in creating immersive VR experiences for the Oculus Rift, Oculus Quest, and other Oculus headsets. For example, in VR games like *Beat Saber*, developers use Unity to create the 3D environments, interactive objects, and real-time player

97

interactions, all while ensuring smooth performance and immersion in VR.

---

2. Unreal Engine: High-Fidelity 3D Worlds for the Metaverse

Unreal Engine (UE) is known for its high-quality graphics, sophisticated rendering tools, and advanced physics engine. While Unity is often preferred for its versatility and ease of use, Unreal Engine stands out for creating visually stunning, high-fidelity environments. It's the engine of choice for developers aiming to push the limits of graphics and realism, especially in large-scale virtual worlds that require high performance and photorealistic rendering.

- **Core Features of Unreal Engine for Metaverse Development**:
  - **Photorealistic Graphics**: Unreal Engine is renowned for its **high-quality rendering capabilities**, including support for **ray tracing** and **real-time lighting**. This allows developers to create virtual worlds that look incredibly realistic, with lifelike textures, dynamic lighting, and intricate detail. Unreal Engine's graphics quality makes it a top choice for applications that require realism, such as virtual real estate tours or architectural visualizations.

- o **Blueprint Visual Scripting**: Unreal Engine uses **Blueprint**, a visual scripting system that allows developers to create game mechanics, interactions, and events without writing code. This system is particularly useful for designers and artists who want to implement interactive features without extensive programming knowledge.

- o **Advanced Physics and AI**: Unreal Engine's built-in physics system allows for realistic simulations of real-world behavior, including gravity, object collisions, and fluid dynamics. Additionally, Unreal's **AI framework** is robust, allowing developers to create complex, reactive NPCs (Non-Player Characters) that can interact with users in meaningful ways.

- o **VR and AR Support**: Unreal Engine supports a wide range of VR and AR devices, from **Oculus Rift** and **HTC Vive** to **Magic Leap** and **Microsoft HoloLens**. Unreal Engine allows for the creation of high-performance VR experiences, enabling developers to create immersive environments that run smoothly on various platforms.

- **Real-world   Example**: **Fortnite**, one of the most popular games in the world, is built using Unreal Engine. The game's success can be attributed to its visually stunning environments, advanced physics, and seamless multiplayer interaction. Unreal Engine's ability to handle large, complex 3D worlds with high-quality graphics and smooth gameplay is what makes *Fortnite* stand out. In addition, the game's frequent updates and events, like in-game concerts or crossovers, demonstrate the engine's capability to create dynamic, ever-evolving virtual worlds, which are a hallmark of Metaverse experiences.

3. The Role of Game Engines in Metaverse Development

Game engines like **Unity** and **Unreal Engine** are the primary tools for building virtual worlds within the Metaverse. Both platforms provide the foundational elements needed to create complex, interactive environments. These engines enable developers to build not only the 3D spaces but also the systems and mechanics that make the virtual world engaging.

- **Real-time Interaction**: Both Unity and Unreal Engine provide real-time rendering capabilities, which are essential for creating interactive, dynamic virtual worlds. Whether users are exploring a digital landscape, interacting with objects, or socializing with others, real-time interaction is crucial for a seamless experience.

100

- **Multiplayer Support**: Both engines offer built-in tools for creating multiplayer environments, allowing developers to create persistent worlds where users can interact with one another in real-time. Whether it's a game, a virtual office, or a social platform, both Unity and Unreal support multiplayer mechanics, chat systems, and user-driven content.

- **Asset Management**: Efficiently managing assets like 3D models, textures, and animations is vital in virtual world development. Both Unity and Unreal Engine offer asset management tools that allow developers to organize and import content from external sources. This speeds up development by allowing teams to reuse assets and iterate on designs more quickly.

- **Optimization and Performance**: The Metaverse will require virtual worlds that can handle large numbers of users interacting simultaneously. Both Unity and Unreal Engine provide optimization tools to ensure that virtual worlds perform well, even with high user traffic. Developers can adjust settings to maintain smooth performance without sacrificing visual quality, ensuring that users have a pleasant experience regardless of their device.

4. WebXR: Extending the Metaverse to the Browser

While Unity and Unreal Engine are primarily used for creating downloadable applications, **WebXR** is the technology that enables virtual worlds to be accessed directly through a web browser. WebXR is an open standard that allows developers to build AR and VR experiences that work seamlessly on browsers like Chrome and Firefox.

- **Core Features of WebXR**:
    - **Cross-Device Support**: WebXR experiences can be accessed through a variety of devices, including desktop computers, mobile phones, and VR/AR headsets. This makes WebXR a great tool for creating Metaverse experiences that are easily accessible without requiring users to download special applications.
    - **Simplicity and Accessibility**: WebXR makes it easier for users to access virtual worlds without the need for specialized hardware. It's perfect for lightweight virtual spaces, demos, and environments that don't require high levels of detail or performance.
- **Real-world** **Example**: While not as advanced as Unity or Unreal in terms of graphical fidelity, **WebXR** enables browsers to host simple Metaverse-style experiences. For example, a

WebXR experience might allow users to explore an art gallery in VR or engage in a virtual shopping experience without leaving their browser. Platforms like **Mozilla Hubs** use WebXR to create virtual spaces that users can access directly through their web browser, offering a convenient and accessible entry point into the Metaverse.

Conclusion

Game engines like **Unity** and **Unreal Engine** are essential for creating the virtual worlds of the Metaverse, each offering unique strengths that help bring immersive, interactive environments to life. Unity's flexibility and cross-platform compatibility make it ideal for a wide variety of virtual experiences, from VR games to simulations. Unreal Engine, with its high-fidelity rendering capabilities and advanced physics, is perfect for creating realistic, high-performance virtual worlds.

As the Metaverse continues to grow, these game engines will be key in shaping the future of digital spaces. They enable developers to craft detailed, engaging environments that users can explore, interact with, and inhabit, paving the way for the next generation of virtual worlds.

In the next chapter, we will explore **building interactive systems and game mechanics** within these virtual worlds, including how to create user-driven content, multiplayer experiences, and responsive environments that enhance immersion and engagement.

CHAPTER 11

SCRIPTING AND PROGRAMMING IN VIRTUAL WORLDS

Overview: An Introduction to Programming Languages and Scripting Within the Context of Virtual World Creation (e.g., C# for Unity, Blueprints for Unreal Engine)

Creating interactive and dynamic virtual worlds goes beyond the visual elements of 3D models and textures. Scripting and programming are essential components that allow developers to add interactivity, behavior, and functionality to these worlds. Whether it's controlling the movement of avatars, managing game logic, or creating complex environmental interactions, programming languages and scripting systems are key to making virtual worlds engaging and interactive.

In this chapter, we will explore the scripting and programming aspects of virtual world development, focusing on common languages and tools used in platforms like **Unity** and **Unreal Engine**. We will discuss how developers write code to create interactive experiences, and how visual scripting tools like **Blueprints** in Unreal Engine can make programming more accessible to non-programmers. Additionally, we'll examine how scripting is applied in real-world examples, such as **VRChat** and **Roblox**, to bring virtual worlds to life.

---

1. Scripting and Programming for Virtual Worlds

Scripting and programming in virtual world development can range from simple interactions, such as picking up objects, to complex systems, such as multiplayer support, AI behaviors, and physics simulations. Different game engines use various languages and systems for scripting, each suited to the unique needs of the developer and the type of virtual world being created.

- **Unity Scripting with C#**: Unity uses **C#** as its primary programming language for creating gameplay systems, interactions, and user interfaces. C# is a powerful, object-oriented language that is easy to learn, making it a popular choice for developers of all skill levels. With C#, developers can control character movement, create interactions with objects, manage game states, and implement complex features like multiplayer and inventory systems.
  - **Key Features of C# for Unity**:
    - **Object-Oriented Programming (OOP)**: C# is based on OOP, meaning it organizes code around objects and the actions they can perform. This makes it

106

easier to manage complex systems and create reusable components.

- **MonoBehaviour**: Unity's base class for all scripts. It provides essential methods like `Start()`, `Update()`, and `Awake()`, which are automatically called during gameplay, allowing for real-time interaction and control.

- **Unity's API**: Unity provides a rich set of APIs (Application Programming Interfaces) that allow developers to access and manipulate game objects, physics, and rendering directly.

  o **Real-world** **Example**: In *VRChat*, developers use C# to script interactive environments and avatars. For instance, avatars can be scripted to perform specific actions like dancing, triggering sound effects, or changing their appearance based on in-game events or user input. C# scripts are also used to define the behavior of interactive objects, such as doors, buttons, or puzzles, creating a rich, engaging experience for users.

- **Unreal Engine's Blueprints Visual Scripting**: Unlike Unity, which uses C#, Unreal Engine offers **Blueprints**, a visual scripting language that allows developers to create gameplay logic and interactions without writing any code. Blueprint scripting is ideal for designers and artists who may not have extensive programming experience but still want to implement complex systems.

- ○ **Key Features of Blueprints for Unreal Engine**:
  - ▪ **Visual Interface**: Blueprints provide a node-based interface, where developers connect "nodes" representing actions, conditions, and variables. This makes programming more intuitive by visually representing game logic and interactions.
  - ▪ **Real-Time Feedback**: Blueprint scripting allows developers to see changes immediately, making it ideal for rapid prototyping and iteration.
  - ▪ **Powerful Event-Driven System**: Unreal Engine's event-driven system allows Blueprints to respond to user input, environmental changes, and game states. It's a great way to create interactive experiences that react dynamically to player behavior.
  - ▪ **Extensibility with C++**: For more complex tasks, Blueprint can be extended using C++, giving developers the

flexibility to use both visual and written programming methods.

- o **Real-world** **Example**: *Fortnite* is a prime example of how Unreal Engine's Blueprint system is used to create interactive and dynamic gameplay mechanics. Blueprint scripting is used to create the behavior of weapons, power-ups, and even environmental events like storm changes or in-game challenges. The system allows developers to quickly design new features, such as temporary gameplay modes or events, without needing to write complex code.

2. Programming for Interactivity in Virtual Worlds

Creating interactive experiences is one of the primary goals of virtual world development. Scripting allows users to interact with objects, NPCs (non-player characters), and the environment in meaningful ways. In a virtual world, interactions are driven by **events**, **triggers**, and **conditions** set by the developer.

- • **User** **Interactions** **and** **Input**: In both Unity and Unreal Engine, developers use scripting to handle user inputs, such as mouse clicks, keyboard presses, touch gestures, and VR controller movements.

This allows users to manipulate objects, move avatars, or trigger actions within the world.

- o **Unity**: Using C#, developers can use Unity's Input API to manage user inputs, allowing the player to interact with the environment or other players.

- o **Unreal Engine**: With Blueprints, developers can create visual scripts to handle user inputs, such as triggering a door to open when the player presses a button or interacting with an NPC to initiate a conversation.

- **Events and Triggers**: Events and triggers are essential for creating dynamic, reactive environments. Developers can script specific actions that occur when a user interacts with an object or enters a particular area of the virtual world.

  - o **Unity**: Using C#, developers can create **colliders** that detect when the player enters a zone, triggering specific events, such as activating an elevator or starting a quest.

  - o **Unreal Engine**: Blueprints allow for the creation of triggers and events, such as door-opening animations when the player approaches or triggering environmental effects when a specific condition is met.

- **NPC and AI Behaviors**: Programming NPCs and AI (artificial intelligence) behaviors is a critical aspect of virtual world development. Scripting can be used to make NPCs react to player actions, follow specific behaviors, or participate in world events.

  o **Unity**: Using C# scripts, developers can create NPCs with behaviors like patrolling, chasing, or following the player. Unity's **NavMesh** system can be used to define AI navigation paths.

  o **Unreal Engine**: In Unreal, AI behavior is controlled through Blueprints or C++, using tools like **Behavior Trees** to define NPC actions and decision-making processes.

---

3. Scripting for Virtual Reality and Sandbox Games

In virtual reality (VR) and sandbox-style games, scripting is particularly important because it allows for more immersive and interactive experiences. VR introduces unique challenges, such as handling user movement and managing physical interactions, while sandbox games often give users the freedom to create and manipulate objects and environments.

- **Scripting for VR**: In VR, developers need to account for user movements, interactions, and object manipulation in three-dimensional space. VR-specific input, such as hand controllers, gaze tracking, and motion detection, requires scripting to make these actions feel natural and responsive.

- o **Unity for VR**: Unity provides VR SDKs (software development kits) for platforms like **Oculus**, **HTC Vive**, and **PlayStation VR**. Developers can use C# to handle input from VR controllers, create interactive environments, and manage user movement in the virtual world.

- o **Unreal Engine for VR**: Unreal's Blueprint system allows developers to script VR interactions visually, making it easier to design complex interactions like object grabbing, throwing, or teleporting.

- **Scripting in Sandbox Games like Roblox**: In sandbox games like **Roblox**, users can create their own worlds, customize avatars, and design game mechanics. Roblox uses **Lua**, a lightweight scripting language, to allow users to create interactive content and game systems.

  - o **Real-world Example**: In *Roblox*, Lua scripting is used extensively to allow players to build custom worlds, implement game mechanics, and create unique gameplay experiences. Developers use Lua to script everything from simple user interactions (like opening a door) to complex game systems (like in-game currency or combat mechanics). The flexibility of Lua allows for a wide range of creativity and functionality in the Roblox Metaverse.

Conclusion

Scripting and programming are essential components of virtual world creation, enabling developers to bring interactivity, logic, and user engagement to their environments. Whether through **C#** in Unity, **Blueprints** in Unreal Engine, or **Lua** in Roblox, the scripting tools available to developers allow for the creation of dynamic, responsive, and engaging virtual worlds.

From managing user input to controlling NPC behavior, scripting gives developers the power to design interactive experiences that immerse users in the Metaverse. As demonstrated by examples like *VRChat* and *Roblox*, scripting plays a vital role in enabling users to interact with and influence the virtual world.

In the next chapter, we will explore **multiplayer functionality and networking** within virtual worlds, focusing on how developers can enable real-time interactions and create persistent environments for users to share and experience together.

CHAPTER 12

BUILDING MULTIPLAYER EXPERIENCES

Overview: Techniques and Protocols for Developing Multiplayer Interactions and Networking in Virtual Worlds

One of the defining features of the Metaverse is the ability for multiple users to interact with each other in real-time within shared virtual spaces. Creating these multiplayer experiences involves designing systems that enable users to communicate, collaborate, and engage with one another seamlessly. This requires a deep understanding of networking protocols, server architecture, and synchronization techniques to ensure smooth, lag-free interactions and a cohesive virtual world.

In this chapter, we will explore the key techniques and protocols that developers use to build multiplayer interactions in virtual worlds. We will cover the networking principles behind real-time communication, synchronization of game states, and the importance of server-client models. Additionally, we will look at real-world examples, such as the multiplayer mechanics in **VRChat** and the network architecture of **Fortnite**, to see how these concepts are applied in large-scale virtual worlds.

1. Understanding Multiplayer Networking in Virtual Worlds

Networking in virtual worlds is essential for enabling users to interact with one another in real-time. Multiplayer games and social platforms must rely on robust networking systems that manage the communication between clients (players) and servers (the game or platform's host). Understanding the basic components of multiplayer networking is crucial for building any multiplayer experience.

- **Client-Server Architecture**:
  The most common model for multiplayer games and virtual worlds is the **client-server** architecture, where the server acts as the central hub, managing game logic, storing data, and ensuring all clients (users) are synchronized. The client (typically the user's computer or device) sends requests to the server, and the server processes these requests, updates the game state, and sends responses back to the clients.

  o **Server-Authoritative Models**: In this model, the server has the final say over the game state, and clients are kept in sync by the server's authoritative updates. This model ensures that there is no cheating or inconsistent gameplay, as all important decisions are made by the server.

116

- o **Peer-to-Peer Models**: In this architecture, players communicate directly with one another without a central server. Peer-to-peer networking is often used for smaller-scale multiplayer experiences or games that do not require heavy server-side processing. However, this model can lead to inconsistencies and latency issues, especially when players are located far apart.

- **Networking   Protocols**: Multiplayer interactions require efficient protocols to transfer data between clients and servers. Some common networking protocols used in virtual world development include:

  - o **TCP/IP   (Transmission   Control Protocol/Internet Protocol)**: A reliable protocol for sending data packets. TCP ensures that data arrives in order and without errors, making it suitable for less time-sensitive interactions (like chat or object updates).

  - o **UDP (User Datagram Protocol)**: A faster, less reliable protocol often used for real-time multiplayer interactions, where speed is crucial, and occasional data loss is acceptable. UDP is commonly used in games and VR experiences because of its low latency, which is critical for real-time communication.

117

o **WebSockets**: A protocol that enables full-duplex communication channels over a single TCP connection. WebSockets are useful for real-time, bidirectional communication in virtual worlds, especially in browser-based games and applications.

2. Synchronization and State Management in Multiplayer Worlds

One of the most challenging aspects of multiplayer game development is maintaining synchronization between all players in a shared virtual space. Virtual worlds often require constant updates to ensure that every player sees the same state at the same time. This involves synchronizing player movements, object states, and interactions.

- **State   Synchronization**: In multiplayer games, the game state must be consistent across all clients. This means that when one player moves, jumps, or interacts with an object, that change must be reflected on all other players' screens. This is typically done through regular **state updates** sent from the server to the clients.
    o **Delta Compression**: To reduce bandwidth usage and improve performance, only the changes (or deltas) in the game state are sent to the clients.

118

For example, instead of sending the entire position of an avatar each time, the server might only send the change in the avatar's position (e.g., "moved 5 meters to the right").

- **Lag Compensation**: Since internet connections are rarely perfect, there is always some level of latency or lag in multiplayer games. Developers must implement systems to compensate for lag, such as **client-side prediction**, where the client predicts what will happen next and updates the user's game state accordingly, while the server sends corrections as needed.

- **Event   Handling**: Multiplayer virtual worlds often use **event-driven programming** to handle interactions. Events, such as player actions or system updates, trigger changes in the game state. For example, when one player opens a door in a virtual world, the server sends an event that updates all players' states to reflect the change. These events are sent through networking protocols and are processed by the client to update the environment accordingly.

- **Real-time Synchronization Techniques**:
  - **Lockstep Simulation**: This technique ensures that all clients are running the same simulation at the same time by synchronizing the game state across all devices. Each player's inputs are sent

to the server, and the server broadcasts the resulting state to all players, ensuring a uniform experience.

o **Interpolation and Extrapolation**: These techniques are used to smooth out the movement of players and objects when there is network lag. **Interpolation** estimates the positions of players based on the data received from the server, while **extrapolation** predicts future movements, helping to create a smooth experience despite latency.

3. Real-world Example: Multiplayer Mechanics in VRChat

VRChat is a popular social platform in the Metaverse that allows users to explore virtual environments, create custom avatars, and interact with other users in real-time. The multiplayer mechanics in VRChat are crucial for creating the immersive social experience that users enjoy.

- **Avatar   Synchronization**: In **VRChat**, one of the most important features is the synchronization of avatars. When one user moves or interacts with their avatar, the changes must be reflected in real-time across all other users' screens. This is achieved using Unity and networking protocols, where the movement data for avatars is continuously updated and sent to the server, which then distributes the updated data to all clients. This ensures that all users see the same actions and movements in real-time.

- **Voice and Gesture Communication**: **VRChat** also uses spatial audio to enhance communication between users. As players move closer to one another, their voices become louder, and as they move farther away, the sound diminishes. This is an example of **spatial synchronization** in multiplayer virtual worlds. The system also uses gestures and body movements to create more engaging social interactions, which are captured using VR controllers and sensors.

- **Multiplayer Spaces**: VRChat offers dynamic multiplayer worlds where users can explore together, play games, or attend virtual events. The platform relies on Unity's networking tools to manage the multiplayer environment, ensuring that users can seamlessly join and leave worlds, interact with objects, and collaborate on activities with little to no lag.

4. Real-world Example: Network Architecture of Massive Open Worlds like Fortnite

Fortnite is one of the largest and most popular multiplayer online games, and its success hinges on its ability to handle massive numbers of players interacting in a shared world. The network architecture behind Fortnite is designed to handle **real-time multiplayer interactions** and deliver a smooth experience for millions of users worldwide.

- **Matchmaking and Server Allocation**: Fortnite uses a dynamic matchmaking system that assigns players to servers based on their geographic location and skill level. By using distributed servers, Epic Games can ensure that players are matched with others who have similar ping times, minimizing latency and improving overall gameplay quality.

- **Persistent World and Real-Time Events**: Fortnite's world is dynamic and constantly evolving, with regular in-game events, such as limited-time modes or seasonal updates. The game's **persistent world** is managed by a set of servers that store player data and world states, allowing users to return to the game and pick up where they left off. Events and updates are broadcast to all players in real-time, ensuring that everyone in the world experiences the same changes simultaneously.

- **Data Centers and Edge Servers**: Fortnite relies on **data centers** and **edge servers** to handle the enormous load of concurrent players. By placing servers in various geographic locations, Epic Games ensures that players experience minimal latency, regardless of where they are located. Edge servers also help reduce the load on the central servers by caching frequently accessed data, further improving performance.

Conclusion

Building multiplayer experiences in virtual worlds is one of the most complex yet rewarding challenges for developers. By understanding the fundamentals of **client-server architecture**, **network protocols**, and **synchronization techniques**, developers can create seamless, real-time interactions that enable users to connect and interact in meaningful ways.

As seen in **VRChat** and **Fortnite**, the ability to handle large-scale multiplayer interactions and synchronize game states is key to building engaging, persistent virtual worlds. In the next chapter, we will dive into **multiplayer game mechanics**, exploring how developers can design engaging and dynamic experiences that keep players immersed and interacting within these virtual environments.

CHAPTER 13

BLOCKCHAIN AND VIRTUAL OWNERSHIP

Overview: Exploring How Blockchain is Used to Verify Ownership, Digital Assets, and Currency in the Metaverse

As the Metaverse evolves, so does the concept of ownership within these digital spaces. While physical items are governed by traditional systems of ownership and property laws, virtual assets, items, and currencies in the Metaverse require a new model of verification. **Blockchain technology** provides a decentralized and secure way to verify ownership, track digital assets, and facilitate transactions in virtual worlds. Through its transparency and immutability, blockchain enables users to own, buy, and sell digital goods with confidence.

In this chapter, we will explore how blockchain technology plays a vital role in establishing **virtual ownership**, including its use in verifying ownership of **digital assets** and **virtual currencies**. We'll look at how **Non-Fungible Tokens (NFTs)** have revolutionized the concept of digital ownership in virtual worlds like **Decentraland** and **Cryptovoxels**, and how these technologies contribute to the overall Metaverse economy.

1. Understanding Blockchain and Virtual Ownership

At its core, blockchain is a distributed ledger technology that allows data to be securely stored across multiple computers or nodes, ensuring that records of transactions or ownership are immutable and transparent. In the context of the Metaverse, blockchain serves as a digital registry where ownership of virtual assets can be verified and transferred without the need for central authorities or intermediaries.

- **Decentralization**:

    One of the key features of blockchain is its **decentralized nature**. Unlike traditional databases, which rely on a central authority (such as a bank or a government), blockchain operates on a peer-to-peer network where no single entity controls the system. This decentralization makes blockchain particularly well-suited for virtual worlds, where trust and transparency are essential for users to feel secure in their digital interactions.

- **Immutability**:

    Once a transaction or piece of information is recorded on the blockchain, it cannot be altered or erased. This property of **immutability** ensures that ownership records are permanent and tamper-proof, making blockchain ideal for verifying digital ownership. Whether it's a virtual piece of land, a digital artwork, or an avatar, the proof of ownership is securely recorded on the blockchain.

- **Tokenization**:

  Blockchain allows for the **tokenization** of digital assets, turning them into unique, tradeable items. Through **smart contracts**, developers can create digital items that are owned, transferred, and traded with verifiable ownership. These tokens can represent a wide variety of assets, from virtual land and clothing in virtual worlds to collectible items and artworks in the form of NFTs.

---

2. The Role of NFTs (Non-Fungible Tokens) in Virtual Ownership

NFTs (Non-Fungible Tokens) have become a major innovation in the Metaverse, providing a way to establish verifiable digital ownership. Unlike cryptocurrencies like Bitcoin or Ethereum, which are **fungible** (interchangeable with each other), NFTs are **unique**, each representing a distinct digital asset. This uniqueness makes NFTs ideal for representing ownership of virtual items, art, land, or even moments within virtual worlds.

- **What Makes NFTs Different**:
  - o **Unique and Indivisible**: Each NFT is unique and cannot be divided into smaller units like cryptocurrencies. This means each NFT represents a one-of-a-kind item, such as a digital

painting, an in-game item, or a piece of virtual land.

- o **Verifiable Ownership**: NFTs are recorded on a blockchain, providing a transparent and secure way to prove ownership. The blockchain serves as a public ledger, allowing anyone to verify the ownership history of an NFT, whether it's a piece of art, a virtual property, or a collectible item.

- o **Smart Contracts**: NFTs are often associated with **smart contracts**, which are self-executing contracts with the terms of the agreement directly written into code. Smart contracts facilitate the automatic transfer of ownership when conditions are met, such as when a buyer purchases an NFT from a seller. These contracts make transactions secure and efficient.

- **Real-world   Example**:
Decentraland, a virtual world built on the Ethereum blockchain, allows users to purchase, sell, and trade virtual land parcels using NFTs. Each piece of land in Decentraland is represented as an NFT, and users can freely buy and sell these parcels within the platform or on secondary markets. The ownership of each virtual land parcel is secured and verified through the Ethereum blockchain, ensuring that users have true ownership of their assets.

Similarly, **Cryptovoxels** is another virtual world where users can buy, sell, and build on virtual land. Like Decentraland, Cryptovoxels uses NFTs to represent ownership of parcels of land, allowing for seamless transfers of property between users. NFTs in Cryptovoxels can also be used for creating and trading art, wearables, and other digital assets within the world.

3. Blockchain-Based Digital Currencies and Virtual Economies

In addition to NFTs, **digital currencies** (often based on blockchain) are another key aspect of virtual worlds in the Metaverse. These virtual currencies are used to buy, sell, and trade virtual assets, and they often act as the primary medium of exchange within a platform's economy.

- **Cryptocurrencies and Virtual Currencies**: Virtual worlds and Metaverse platforms typically have their own digital currencies that are used for transactions within the world. These currencies are often based on blockchain technology and can be exchanged for real-world currencies (e.g., **Bitcoin**, **Ethereum**, **USDT**) or other virtual assets. For example, **Decentraland** has its own native cryptocurrency, **MANA**, which is used for purchasing land, items, and services within the platform.

- o **MANA**: Users can purchase MANA using real-world currency, and then use it to buy virtual goods, land, or services within the Decentraland ecosystem. The currency operates on the Ethereum blockchain, making transactions transparent and secure.

- o **Sandbox**: Similarly, **The Sandbox**, another virtual world built on blockchain, uses its native currency, **SAND**, to buy land, participate in the game economy, and engage with other players. SAND can be bought, traded, or used within the game, and transactions are all verified through blockchain technology.

- **Tokenized Economies and Ownership**: Virtual worlds that use blockchain also enable users to participate in tokenized economies, where not only land and assets are tokenized as NFTs, but also game mechanics, art, and experiences. For example, players can earn **tokenized rewards** or buy **virtual goods** with blockchain-based tokens. This creates a more robust economic ecosystem where users can create, sell, and trade assets directly with one another, all while maintaining verifiable ownership.

4. The Future of Virtual Ownership and Blockchain in the Metaverse

The integration of blockchain and NFTs into the Metaverse is still in its early stages, but it is clear that they will play a fundamental role in how digital ownership, assets, and currencies are structured in virtual worlds.

- **Interoperability Between Virtual Worlds**: One of the most exciting possibilities of blockchain technology in the Metaverse is **interoperability**. The idea is that users can take their assets, such as NFTs or virtual currency, from one platform to another. For example, an avatar's outfit or a digital artwork purchased in one virtual world could be used or displayed in another. Blockchain provides the foundation for this cross-platform compatibility, as assets are stored on decentralized ledgers that are accessible from multiple virtual environments.

- **Virtual Property Ownership as Real Estate**: Virtual property ownership, powered by blockchain, could become as valuable as real-world real estate. Platforms like Decentraland and Cryptovoxels already allow users to buy, sell, and develop virtual land, but as more industries and individuals invest in virtual spaces, the value of these assets may rise significantly. Virtual real estate could be used for business, entertainment, or even social gatherings, creating an entirely new market for virtual property and services.

- **User-Generated Content and Intellectual Property**: Blockchain also allows creators to establish true ownership of their digital creations. Artists, developers, and designers can tokenize their content, ensuring that they retain control over how it is used, traded, and monetized. For example, a musician can release music as an NFT and ensure that the buyer has exclusive rights to the track, and the creator can receive royalties each time the NFT is resold.

Conclusion

Blockchain technology and **Non-Fungible Tokens (NFTs)** are revolutionizing the way ownership is understood and verified in the Metaverse. By providing secure, transparent, and immutable records of ownership, blockchain has enabled a new model of digital ownership for virtual assets, land, and currencies. This system not only empowers creators and users but also fosters trust in the virtual economy, allowing for true ownership of digital goods.

Platforms like **Decentraland** and **Cryptovoxels** are leading the way by using NFTs to secure ownership of virtual property, while cryptocurrencies like **MANA** and **SAND** facilitate in-world transactions. As the Metaverse expands, blockchain will continue to be at the core of its economic structure, creating new opportunities for digital commerce, art, and interaction.

In the next chapter, we will explore **virtual economies and marketplaces**, diving deeper into how the buying, selling, and trading of digital goods and services are shaping the future of the Metaverse.

CHAPTER 14

MONETIZATION STRATEGIES FOR VIRTUAL WORLDS

Overview: Explore Various Monetization Strategies Including In-App Purchases, Subscriptions, Virtual Goods, and Advertising

As the Metaverse continues to expand, virtual worlds are becoming not just a space for entertainment and social interaction but also a significant economic ecosystem. Developers and creators can leverage various monetization strategies to generate revenue from their virtual worlds, whether through in-game purchases, subscriptions, virtual goods, or advertising. These strategies not only help sustain the virtual economy but also provide opportunities for creators and businesses to profit from their digital assets and content.

In this chapter, we will explore the key monetization strategies used in virtual worlds and the Metaverse, examining how they work and how they benefit both developers and users. We will also look at real-world examples, such as how **Fortnite** and **Roblox** utilize in-game purchases and virtual currencies to generate significant revenue, while providing value to players and creators.

1. In-App Purchases and Microtransactions

One of the most common and successful monetization strategies for virtual worlds is **in-app purchases** or **microtransactions**. These allow players to purchase virtual items, services, or benefits within the game or virtual environment, often in exchange for real-world currency.

- **Cosmetic   Items**:
  In virtual worlds, many in-app purchases involve **cosmetic items** that alter the appearance of avatars, skins, outfits, or other visual elements without affecting gameplay. For instance, players may purchase exclusive skins, outfits, or emotes to customize their avatars, making them unique and distinct from others.

- **Power-ups   and   Boosts**:
  Some virtual worlds monetize by offering **power-ups**, **boosts**, or temporary advantages that enhance gameplay. These can include things like extra lives, faster movement, or access to exclusive areas. These purchases often provide players with a way to progress faster or gain an edge in the game, but they don't necessarily affect the core mechanics of the game, ensuring the experience remains balanced.

- **Season   Passes**:
  Many virtual worlds and games now offer **season passes**,

where players can pay for a bundle of content that is unlocked over time. This could include exclusive cosmetics, challenges, or access to special events. Season passes create a sense of urgency and encourage users to engage with the platform regularly, as new content becomes available.

- **Real-world Example: Fortnite**: *Fortnite*, developed by Epic Games, is one of the most successful games in the world, primarily due to its **in-app purchases** model. The game is free to play, but players can purchase virtual currency called **V-bucks**. V-bucks are used to buy a variety of in-game cosmetics, such as skins, dances, and emotes for avatars, as well as special items during events. **Fortnite's Battle Pass** also follows the season-based model, giving players access to exclusive rewards and unlockables through the purchase of a season pass. This strategy has been immensely profitable, generating billions of dollars in revenue.

2. Subscriptions and Premium Content

Another popular monetization strategy in the Metaverse is the use of **subscriptions** or premium membership models. These offer users exclusive content, perks, or experiences in exchange for regular payments. Subscriptions help developers generate consistent, recurring revenue while providing subscribers with added value.

- **Premium   Membership**: A subscription-based model typically involves offering users a premium version of the game or virtual world, where they receive exclusive access to content, experiences, or features. Premium members may receive early access to new content, special rewards, or enhanced functionality, such as the ability to customize avatars or build in virtual environments more freely.

- **Access   to   Exclusive   Areas**: Subscriptions can also give users access to **exclusive areas** or **VIP zones** within the virtual world, where they can participate in special events, challenges, or social experiences that regular users cannot access.

- **Real-world   Example: Roblox**: *Roblox* employs a subscription model known as the **Roblox Premium** membership. Premium members receive a monthly allocation of **Robux** (the platform's virtual currency), which they can use to buy in-game items, purchase customizations for avatars, and access premium games and experiences within the Roblox ecosystem. Premium members also get the ability to sell items and games, allowing them to monetize their own content. This subscription model has helped Roblox generate consistent revenue, supporting the platform's growth.

---

3. Virtual Goods and Asset Sales

Selling **virtual goods** and digital assets is another effective way to generate revenue within virtual worlds. These goods can range from simple cosmetic items (like clothing or skins) to more complex assets (like virtual land, objects, and buildings).

- **Digital Land and Property**: In many virtual worlds, land and property are tokenized as **NFTs** (Non-Fungible Tokens) and can be bought, sold, and traded. Virtual land in platforms like **Decentraland** or **The Sandbox** is sold as NFTs, allowing users to purchase their own space in the virtual world. These assets can be developed, customized, and even rented or sold to other users, creating an entire virtual real estate market.

- **Marketplace for User-Generated Content**: Many virtual worlds, particularly those built on blockchain, allow users to create and sell their own virtual goods. This can include 3D models, virtual clothing, accessories, and even artworks. These platforms create a marketplace where users can monetize their creativity and earn income from their designs.

- **Real-world Example: Decentraland**: In *Decentraland*, users can purchase virtual land represented as NFTs using **MANA**, the platform's cryptocurrency. Once purchased, users can build or develop on their virtual land, create stores, host events, or even display digital art. The ability to buy and sell virtual property has made Decentraland one of the leading virtual worlds in terms of virtual real estate investments. Users can also buy and sell digital goods, such as clothing and art, in the Decentraland marketplace.

---

4. Advertising in the Metaverse

As virtual worlds continue to grow in popularity, they are becoming new spaces for **advertising** and **sponsorships**. Brands are eager to reach the virtual audience, and virtual worlds provide a unique platform for interactive, immersive ads.

- **In-World Advertising**: Virtual worlds can incorporate digital billboards, product placements, or branded experiences. These ads can appear in high-traffic areas within the virtual world, such as popular event spaces, social hubs, or virtual malls. Advertisers can create interactive experiences where users engage with the brand, play branded mini-games, or even receive rewards for interacting with the ad.

- **Sponsorships**:

  Some virtual worlds host sponsored events, competitions, or in-game items that promote a brand. For instance, a virtual concert might be sponsored by a major beverage company, or a limited-time skin might be designed in collaboration with a fashion brand. These sponsored events not only promote the brand but also create unique, memorable experiences for users.

- **Real-world Example: Fortnite**:

  Fortnite has become a pioneer in integrating advertising into virtual worlds. The game regularly collaborates with brands to offer special in-game events and content. For example, Fortnite has hosted in-game concerts by major artists like Travis Scott and Marshmello, with sponsored content and product placements during these events. Additionally, branded skins, such as those based on **Marvel** and **Star Wars**, have generated significant revenue by offering players exclusive, collectible content.

- **Real-world Example: Virtual Billboards in Decentraland**:

  Decentraland has also embraced advertising in its virtual spaces, offering **virtual billboards** where brands can display ads to users. Companies like **Samsung** and **Coca-Cola** have already started advertising in the platform's virtual landscape, helping to create new revenue streams

139

for the platform and enhancing the virtual experience for users with brand engagement.

---

5. Creating a Sustainable Virtual Economy

The success of monetization strategies in virtual worlds largely depends on creating a **sustainable virtual economy**. This economy must balance user experience with revenue generation, ensuring that players and creators remain engaged while still offering opportunities for monetization.

- **Incentivizing Creator Contributions**: Many virtual worlds rely on user-generated content, which means that creators must be incentivized to continue developing assets and content. This can be achieved through revenue-sharing models, where creators earn a percentage of the revenue generated by their creations, whether through virtual goods sales, in-game purchases, or subscriptions.

- **Balancing Pay-to-Play and Free-to-Play**: Finding the right balance between free-to-play access and paid content is essential for keeping the community engaged. Offering valuable content for free while providing opportunities for users to enhance their experience through optional paid content can create a healthy, thriving economy.

140

- **Microtransactions and User Engagement**: Developers must ensure that in-app purchases or microtransactions don't become overly intrusive or hinder the gameplay experience. Ideally, these purchases should provide cosmetic items or enhance the experience without affecting gameplay balance.

Conclusion

Monetization strategies play a crucial role in the development and sustainability of virtual worlds in the Metaverse. Whether through in-app purchases, subscriptions, virtual goods, advertising, or user-generated content, these strategies provide revenue streams that support both developers and users. Platforms like **Fortnite** and **Roblox** have proven that in-game purchases and virtual currencies can create thriving economies, while providing value to players and creators.

As the Metaverse continues to grow, these monetization models will evolve, creating new opportunities for both businesses and individuals to profit from digital assets, content, and experiences. In the next chapter, we will delve into the **challenges and ethical considerations** of monetization in the Metaverse, including issues related to virtual property rights, privacy, and fair trade practices.

CHAPTER 15

VIRTUAL ECONOMY AND VIRTUAL GOODS

Overview: Understanding the Economy of Virtual Worlds, the Concept of Virtual Goods, and How Developers Can Create and Sell Digital Assets

As the Metaverse grows and virtual worlds continue to evolve, one of the most significant aspects of these spaces is the creation and management of **virtual economies**. These digital economies are composed of virtual goods, currencies, and services, and they have begun to mimic real-world economies in many ways. Virtual goods are items or assets that exist solely within a digital environment and can be bought, sold, or traded by users. These goods, which can range from avatars, skins, and art to land and virtual property, are central to the experience of virtual worlds and the broader Metaverse.

In this chapter, we will explore the concept of virtual economies, how virtual goods are created and sold, and the role they play in the overall business model of virtual worlds. We will also examine real-world examples, such as the virtual economy in games like **Second Life** and **Axie Infinity**, which showcase how virtual assets can be bought, sold, and traded for real-world value, often with the help of technologies like **NFTs (Non-Fungible Tokens)**.

---

1. What Is a Virtual Economy?

A **virtual economy** refers to the economic system within a virtual world or digital platform, where goods and services are exchanged, and monetary transactions take place. Unlike traditional economies, where physical goods are bought and sold, virtual economies deal exclusively in **digital goods**—items that exist in a digital or virtual space and are used within the virtual environment.

- **Digital   Currency**:
  Most virtual economies rely on **digital currency** to facilitate transactions. Virtual currencies, like **Robux** in **Roblox** or **V-bucks** in **Fortnite**, are used to buy virtual goods, avatars, skins, or real estate. Some virtual worlds even have their own cryptocurrency-based currencies, such as **MANA** in **Decentraland**.

- **Virtual   Markets**:
  The virtual market consists of platforms and systems where users can trade digital assets. These platforms can be centralized (run by a single company or organization) or decentralized (operating on blockchain technology, which allows for peer-to-peer transactions).

- **Supply and Demand**: Like real-world economies, virtual economies are driven by **supply and demand**. The availability of virtual goods and the number of players seeking them influence their price. Some items become highly sought after and can command significant value, especially if they are rare or limited edition.

- **Real-world Example**: In **Second Life**, a popular virtual world that has existed for over 15 years, the virtual economy is central to the platform's appeal. Users can create, buy, and sell virtual goods such as clothing, furniture, art, and even virtual real estate. **Linden Dollars (L$)** is the currency used within the game, and it can be exchanged for real-world money. Users can build businesses, provide services, and even make a living entirely within the virtual economy of **Second Life**. This economy is driven by user-generated content, and the ability to monetize virtual goods has led to the creation of a thriving marketplace.

2. Virtual Goods: Types and Creation

Virtual goods are digital items that can be bought, sold, or traded within a virtual world. These items are often used to enhance the user's experience, whether by customizing avatars, decorating virtual homes, or unlocking new features within the game.

- **Cosmetic   Items**:
  These items are purely aesthetic and do not affect gameplay mechanics. Examples include **skins, outfits, avatars, emotes**, or **pets**. Cosmetic items are often one of the most popular types of virtual goods, as they allow users to personalize their experience and stand out in the virtual world.

  - o **Real-world Example**: In **Fortnite**, players purchase cosmetics such as skins, gliders, and dances (emotes). These cosmetic items, while purely for aesthetic enjoyment, are a major revenue stream for the game and contribute to the game's massive success. These items are bought using the in-game currency, **V-bucks**, and are constantly updated with seasonal themes and exclusive content.

- **Functional   Items**:
  These items impact gameplay by providing abilities or advantages to the player. They might include **weapons, power-ups, boosters**, or **accessories**. In some cases, functional items are part of the game's progression system and can help players level up or complete missions.

  - o **Real-world Example**: In **World of Warcraft (WoW)**, players can buy items that provide functional benefits, such as **weapons, armor**, or **consumables** (e.g., potions or buffs). While these can be earned through gameplay, many players opt to purchase them through in-game stores or secondary marketplaces.

- **Virtual Real Estate**: Virtual worlds like **Decentraland** or **The Sandbox** offer players the ability to buy, sell, and build on virtual land. These parcels of land are often represented as NFTs, which provide proof of ownership and allow players to build customized structures, host events, or even lease their land to others. Virtual real estate has become a growing market, with some pieces of land being sold for millions of dollars.

  o **Real-world Example**: In **Decentraland**, users can buy and sell virtual land using **MANA**, the platform's native cryptocurrency. These land parcels, represented by NFTs, can be developed into shopping districts, art galleries, or even businesses. Some users even sell or lease virtual spaces for advertising or event hosting, further expanding the economic opportunities within the platform.

3. The Role of NFTs in Virtual Goods and Ownership

NFTs (Non-Fungible Tokens) have revolutionized the concept of ownership within virtual worlds. NFTs are unique digital tokens that represent ownership of a specific asset, and they can be used to prove ownership of virtual goods, land, avatars, and even art. Because NFTs are stored on blockchain networks, they are tamper-proof, transparent, and secure.

- **NFTs as Virtual Assets**: NFTs provide a new way of verifying and transferring ownership of digital goods. Whether it's a virtual painting, a rare collectible, or a piece of land, NFTs allow users to trade and sell items with verifiable proof of ownership.

- **Smart Contracts and Ownership**: NFTs are backed by **smart contracts**, which automatically execute transactions when certain conditions are met. This means that when someone purchases an NFT, the ownership transfer is automatic, ensuring a secure and seamless transaction. The buyer can then choose to keep, sell, or trade the NFT in the future, making NFTs a dynamic part of the virtual economy.

- **Real-world Example: Axie Infinity**: **Axie Infinity**, a blockchain-based game built on Ethereum, allows players to buy, sell, and trade **Axies** (digital pets) and virtual land as NFTs. Players can use their Axies to battle, breed, and earn rewards, and NFTs are used to represent ownership of these digital creatures. The value of Axies fluctuates based on their rarity, stats, and demand, making them highly sought-after virtual assets. Some Axies have sold for thousands of dollars,

147

creating a thriving market of digital pets. This system has transformed the way virtual goods are valued and traded, and it has sparked the rise of blockchain-based gaming economies.

4. Monetizing Virtual Goods: Creation and Sale

Creating and selling virtual goods is an attractive business model for developers and creators in the Metaverse. In order to succeed, developers need to consider what types of goods will resonate with their user base and how they can create a sustainable marketplace. The key is to offer valuable, desirable assets that enhance the virtual world experience.

- **User-Generated Content (UGC)**: Many virtual worlds encourage **user-generated content**, allowing creators to design and sell their own virtual goods. This could include anything from custom avatars and clothing to artwork and game assets. Platforms like **Roblox**, **Second Life**, and **Minecraft** have built thriving economies around user-created content, with creators earning real money from their digital designs.
    - o **Real-world Example: Roblox**: In **Roblox**, players can design and sell **virtual clothing**, **accessories**, and even entire games using the platform's built-in development tools.

Roblox's **DevEx** program allows creators to exchange their virtual earnings for real-world currency, providing a pathway for creators to profit from their work. With millions of active users, Roblox has become a massive marketplace for virtual goods, driving significant revenue for both the platform and its creators.

- **Licensing and Partnerships**: Developers can also create virtual goods by partnering with real-world brands and licensing their intellectual property. For instance, many virtual worlds host branded events or sell limited-edition items that are tied to real-world brands, offering a new revenue stream through **virtual merchandise**.

    o **Real-world Example: Fortnite**: **Fortnite** has created a lucrative marketplace by collaborating with major brands, including **Marvel**, **Star Wars**, **NFL**, and **Travis Scott**, to offer exclusive virtual items and skins. Players can purchase these limited-edition items to customize their avatars and gain access to unique content tied to the brand.

149

Conclusion

Virtual economies and virtual goods have become fundamental components of the Metaverse, providing users with the ability to create, trade, and own digital assets that hold value within these virtual spaces. Whether it's the cosmetic items in **Fortnite**, the virtual land in **Decentraland**, or the collectible Axies in **Axie Infinity**, virtual goods offer new opportunities for monetization and economic growth in the digital world.

As the Metaverse continues to evolve, **NFTs** and **blockchain technology** will play an increasingly important role in verifying ownership and facilitating transactions. The ability to create, buy, and sell virtual assets not only enriches the user experience but also enables developers and creators to build sustainable virtual economies.

In the next chapter, we will explore **virtual marketplaces** and how developers can design and manage platforms where users can buy, sell, and trade virtual goods, unlocking new opportunities for commerce and creativity in the Metaverse.

CHAPTER 16

CREATING AND SELLING DIGITAL ASSETS

Overview: Guide on How Developers and Artists Can Create and Sell Digital Assets (e.g., Avatars, Skins, Furniture, etc.) in Virtual Worlds

The ability to create and sell digital assets has become a significant opportunity for developers and artists in the Metaverse. Virtual worlds and platforms offer a space for creators to design, market, and monetize their work in ways that were previously impossible in traditional environments. Whether it's crafting custom avatars, designing skins, creating furniture, or building virtual buildings, developers and artists now have the tools to create items that not only enhance the virtual world experience but also generate income.

In this chapter, we will guide you through the process of creating digital assets for virtual worlds and provide insight into how to sell them within these environments. We will explore the tools and platforms used to create digital goods, the best practices for developing assets, and the business opportunities available through the creation and sale of virtual goods. Additionally, we will look at real-world examples from platforms like **The**

Sandbox and **Decentraland**, which have pioneered the market for user-generated content and digital asset sales.

---

1. Types of Digital Assets in Virtual Worlds

Before diving into the process of creating and selling digital assets, it's essential to understand the different types of virtual goods that can be created and traded. These digital assets serve various purposes within virtual worlds, from customization to functionality.

- **Avatars and Character Customizations**: Avatars are one of the most common forms of digital assets in virtual worlds. They represent the user's virtual identity and can be customized with skins, clothing, hairstyles, accessories, and animations. Developers can create these assets, either as standalone items or as part of a larger avatar system.
    - o **Example**: In **Roblox**, users can design and sell custom outfits, skins, and accessories for avatars, creating a robust marketplace for digital fashion.
- **Skins and Cosmetics**: **Skins** are a popular category of digital assets, particularly in gaming and virtual worlds. Skins allow users to change the appearance of their characters, weapons, or objects. These assets do not affect gameplay but offer

personalization and aesthetic appeal, making them a popular purchase in free-to-play games.

- o **Example**: **Fortnite** offers a variety of skins, emotes, and back bling that users can purchase with V-bucks. These skins are purely cosmetic but enhance the player's experience by allowing them to stand out in the game.

- **Furniture and Decor**: Virtual furniture and decor are highly sought after in virtual worlds where users can personalize their digital spaces, whether it's in a virtual home, office, or gallery. Artists can design 3D models of chairs, tables, lighting fixtures, and other furniture that users can purchase to enhance their virtual environments.

  - o **Example**: In **Second Life**, users can buy and sell virtual furniture and other in-world items to customize their homes and spaces. Creators can design and upload these items, and users can purchase them using the platform's currency, Linden Dollars.

- **Virtual Land and Real Estate**: Digital real estate, represented as parcels of land in virtual worlds, has become one of the most lucrative forms of digital asset. Developers and users can purchase, build, sell, and lease virtual land within platforms like

Decentraland and **The Sandbox**, offering new opportunities for investment and creativity.

- o **Example**: **The Sandbox** allows users to buy virtual land as NFTs, develop it by building structures, and sell or rent it to others. This creates a thriving market for virtual property, and some land has sold for millions of dollars.

---

2. Tools and Platforms for Creating Digital Assets

To create and sell digital assets, developers and artists need the right tools. These tools enable creators to build 3D models, textures, animations, and interactive elements for use within virtual worlds.

- **3D Modeling Software**: 3D modeling is a key skill for creating digital assets like avatars, furniture, and buildings. Tools like **Blender**, **Maya**, **3ds Max**, and **Cinema 4D** allow creators to model objects in 3D and prepare them for use in virtual worlds. These tools are essential for creating high-quality assets that will be used and purchased by other users.
- **Texturing and Material Creation**: Once 3D models are created, they need textures and materials to make them look realistic or aesthetically pleasing. **Substance Painter** and **Quixel Megascans** are

popular tools used for creating detailed textures and materials that can be applied to 3D models. Textures give depth and detail to models, making them suitable for use in virtual worlds.

- **Animation and Rigging**: If you're creating avatars or objects that need to move (such as animated skins or objects that perform specific actions), animation and rigging are crucial. **Blender**, **Autodesk Maya**, and **Unity** allow developers to rig characters, animate movements, and export the animations for use in virtual worlds.

- **Game Engines**: Many virtual worlds and digital assets are designed within **game engines** like **Unity** and **Unreal Engine**. These engines provide the platform to develop interactive elements, apply physics, and render environments. They also allow developers to integrate assets into the virtual world, program interactivity, and optimize the assets for performance.

- **NFT Creation and Blockchain Platforms**: For creators looking to sell their assets as NFTs, they'll need access to blockchain platforms that support the creation of non-fungible tokens. **OpenSea**, **Rarible**, **Mintable**, and **Foundation** are popular platforms where creators can mint and sell NFTs. Additionally, platforms like **Ethereum**, **Binance Smart Chain**, and **Polygon** provide the blockchain infrastructure for creating and trading NFTs.

---

3. Selling Digital Assets in Virtual Worlds

Once digital assets are created, the next step is to sell them within virtual worlds. There are several strategies for monetizing virtual assets, and each platform has its own system for facilitating transactions.

- **Marketplaces Within Virtual Worlds**: Many virtual worlds and games feature their own built-in marketplaces where creators can upload, showcase, and sell their digital assets. These marketplaces often operate on the platform's native virtual currency, such as **MANA** in **Decentraland** or **Robux** in **Roblox**.
  - o **Real-world Example: Decentraland**: In **Decentraland**, users can create and sell virtual goods, including digital art, wearables, and real estate. The Decentraland marketplace operates with **MANA**, the platform's native cryptocurrency, and creators can set their own prices for their assets. Users can also bid on items or buy them outright, creating a thriving economy of digital goods.

- **NFT** **Marketplaces**: For digital assets like art, avatars, and virtual land that are tokenized as NFTs, creators can sell their items on external NFT marketplaces. These platforms allow creators to mint NFTs representing their assets, sell them to other users, and even earn royalties on future sales of the item.

  - **Real-world Example: The Sandbox**: In **The Sandbox**, users can create and sell digital assets like avatars, skins, and land using NFTs. The platform allows creators to mint their assets as NFTs, and these assets are then sold on **OpenSea**, a popular NFT marketplace. Creators can also earn **SAND** (the platform's native cryptocurrency) by selling or renting their virtual land and goods.

- **Revenue** **Sharing**: Many platforms offer **revenue-sharing models** where creators earn a percentage of the sales from their assets. For example, in **Roblox**, creators earn **Robux** for the items they sell within the game. They can exchange these Robux for real-world currency through Roblox's Developer Exchange (DevEx) program. This model allows developers to monetize their creations and turn their passion for designing virtual goods into a profitable venture.

4. Best Practices for Creating and Selling Digital Assets

To successfully sell digital assets in virtual worlds, creators should keep a few key practices in mind to ensure their items stand out, are valuable, and attract buyers.

- **Understand Your Market**: Before creating assets, it's essential to understand the preferences of your target audience. What kinds of assets are in demand? What styles, themes, or functionalities do users want? Researching popular virtual worlds and studying trends can give you valuable insights into what buyers are looking for.

- **Quality and Detail**: High-quality assets that are well-designed, textured, and functional are more likely to attract buyers. Pay attention to detail, and test your assets in the virtual environment to ensure they work as intended. Well-optimized assets also perform better, reducing lag or crashes in virtual worlds.

- **Collaborate with Other Creators**: Collaborating with other creators can help expand your reach. You might team up with designers, programmers, or game developers to create complex, multi-functional assets that appeal to a wider audience. These collaborations can help generate more visibility for your work and create new business opportunities.

- **Licensing and Copyright**: Be mindful of copyright laws when creating digital assets. If you're using assets that you didn't create yourself (e.g., third-party models, textures, or sounds), make sure you have the proper licenses to use them in your projects. Protecting your intellectual property is essential to ensure you can profit from your work without legal issues.

Conclusion

Creating and selling digital assets is an exciting opportunity for developers and artists in the Metaverse. By understanding the types of digital assets that are in demand, utilizing the right tools for creation, and leveraging marketplaces to sell those assets, creators can generate revenue while enhancing the virtual world experience for users. Platforms like **The Sandbox**, **Decentraland**, and **Roblox** provide ample opportunities for creators to monetize their work and participate in the digital economy.

As virtual worlds continue to evolve, the demand for unique and engaging digital assets will grow. By adhering to best practices and staying informed about trends in the virtual economy, creators can thrive in this new and rapidly expanding marketplace.

In the next chapter, we will explore the role of **virtual services** in the Metaverse, examining how businesses and creators can monetize their time and expertise through services like virtual consulting, event hosting, and digital art creation.

CHAPTER 17

LEGAL AND ETHICAL CONSIDERATIONS IN THE METAVERSE

Overview: Discuss the Legal Challenges in Virtual World Development, Including Intellectual Property, User Rights, and Privacy Concerns

As virtual worlds and the Metaverse continue to expand, they present a wide array of legal and ethical challenges. Unlike traditional digital platforms, virtual worlds are immersive, user-driven environments where the lines between virtual and real-life activities often blur. This creates complex issues related to intellectual property (IP), user rights, privacy, and regulation. Developers and creators must navigate these challenges to ensure their platforms are compliant with laws and that users' rights are respected.

In this chapter, we will discuss the major legal issues that developers face when creating and operating virtual worlds. We will focus on topics like **intellectual property** protection for virtual assets, **user-generated content** (UGC), **privacy** concerns, and **terms of service**. Additionally, we will look at real-world

161

examples, such as the copyright issues surrounding user-created content in **Roblox** and **Fortnite**, to illustrate how these legal challenges play out in practice.

---

1. Intellectual Property (IP) in the Metaverse

Intellectual Property is a broad area of law that protects the creations of the mind, such as designs, inventions, art, music, and literature. In virtual worlds, IP is crucial for protecting digital assets created by developers and users. As virtual environments often feature a wide range of digital goods like avatars, skins, and virtual property, intellectual property rights must be clearly defined to prevent misuse, infringement, or theft.

- **Copyright**:

  Copyright law protects original works of authorship, such as digital art, avatars, music, and code. In the Metaverse, creators may hold the copyright to their assets, giving them the exclusive right to copy, distribute, and sell those assets.

  - **Example**: If a user creates a custom skin for their avatar in **Fortnite** and uploads it to a platform that allows other users to use it, the creator may hold the copyright for that skin, allowing them to control how it is distributed or used. However, issues arise when users upload assets that they did not create, leading to potential copyright infringement.

- **Trademarks**:

  In the Metaverse, brands may create virtual goods or services, such as branded skins, virtual stores, or events. Trademarks protect brand names, logos, and other identifiers that distinguish a product or service in the marketplace.

  - o **Example**: If a clothing brand creates a digital store in **Decentraland** and sells digital clothing items with its logo, it may use trademarks to protect its brand identity and prevent others from using similar logos or designs to mislead users.

- **Patents**:

  Patents protect new inventions or innovative processes. In virtual world development, patents can be used to protect new technologies or unique gaming mechanics, such as methods of virtual interaction or new systems for creating digital assets.

  - o **Example**: If a developer creates a unique system for avatar customization in a virtual world, they could file a patent to protect their technology and prevent others from using the same system without permission.

163

2. User-Generated Content (UGC) and Copyright Issues

One of the defining features of many virtual worlds is **user-generated content**. Platforms like **Roblox, Fortnite**, and **Second Life** allow users to create their own assets, such as avatars, skins, virtual items, and even entire virtual spaces. While this enables creativity and expands the platform's ecosystem, it also raises significant copyright and ownership issues.

- **Ownership of User-Created Content**: When users create content within a platform, the question arises: who owns the content? In many cases, platforms include terms of service agreements that assert the platform retains some rights to user-created content. However, creators often want to retain ownership of their assets, especially if they intend to sell or license them.
  - **Example**: In **Roblox**, users can create and sell virtual goods, such as skins or avatars, within the platform's marketplace. Roblox's terms of service allow the platform to have a certain level of control over these creations, but creators typically retain ownership and can earn **Robux**, the platform's virtual currency. The sale of virtual goods is governed by Roblox's revenue-sharing model, and the platform takes a percentage of the sales.

- **Copyright   Infringement**: In some cases, users may upload content that infringes on the intellectual property of others, either intentionally or unintentionally. This can lead to disputes over ownership and the removal of infringing content from the platform.

  - **Example**: In **Fortnite**, players can create custom skins or items for their avatars. However, there have been instances where users have uploaded skins that resemble copyrighted designs, such as popular movie characters or logos. Epic Games (Fortnite's developer) has faced legal challenges related to user-created content, leading to the removal of infringing items and modifications to their policies to ensure compliance with copyright laws.

- **Licensing   User-Generated   Content**: In some cases, platforms allow creators to license their content to other users or developers, providing a source of income. However, licensing agreements must be clear, ensuring that creators understand how their content can be used and whether they will receive compensation.

  - **Example**: In **The Sandbox**, users can create and sell assets, such as wearables or artwork, using NFTs. These assets are licensed to other players, who can use them within the platform or sell them in the marketplace. Clear licensing agreements ensure that creators are compensated and retain ownership of their work.

---

3. User Rights and Privacy Concerns

As virtual worlds increasingly function as spaces for social interaction, work, and play, **user rights** and **privacy concerns** have become central issues. In the Metaverse, users often share personal information, interact with other players, and create digital identities. These actions raise questions about how personal data is collected, stored, and protected.

- **Data   Privacy**:
  Virtual worlds and Metaverse platforms collect a wide variety of personal data, including names, email addresses, payment information, and behavioral data. Protecting this data from unauthorized access and ensuring that it is used ethically is critical to maintaining user trust.

  - o **Example**: Platforms like **VRChat** and **Decentraland** require users to create accounts that include personal information. If these platforms mishandle user data or fail to comply with data protection laws, they may face legal consequences. The **General Data Protection Regulation (GDPR)** in Europe and other privacy laws worldwide have implications for how virtual worlds manage user data.

- **Digital Identity**: In virtual worlds, users often create digital avatars that represent their identity. Issues related to **identity theft**, **harassment**, and **cyberbullying** are important ethical concerns in these spaces. Developers must ensure that users' digital identities are protected and that they can interact in a safe and respectful environment.

  o **Example**: **Second Life** and **VRChat** have implemented systems to report harassment and block other users to protect players from inappropriate behavior. Ensuring that users can control their digital identities and interactions is essential for creating a positive experience in virtual worlds.

- **Terms of Service and User Agreements**: Every virtual world operates under a set of **terms of service** (TOS) and user agreements that define the rules for participating in the platform. These agreements typically cover user rights, content ownership, and platform responsibilities. It's important for developers to ensure that these agreements are transparent and that users understand their rights and responsibilities within the platform.

167

o **Example**: In **Roblox**, the terms of service explicitly state that the platform owns certain rights to user-generated content uploaded to the platform but also provide guidelines for creators to retain ownership of their creations. The terms also outline how Roblox can use user data and interact with users.

---

4. Regulation and Legal Compliance in Virtual Worlds

As virtual worlds and the Metaverse become more integrated into the global economy, **regulation** and **legal compliance** become increasingly important. Governments around the world are exploring how to regulate digital currencies, virtual assets, and online interactions in virtual spaces.

- **Cryptocurrency and Blockchain Regulation**: As virtual worlds adopt blockchain and cryptocurrency systems, issues of financial regulation come to the forefront. Cryptocurrencies used within virtual economies can raise concerns about fraud, money laundering, and taxation.

  o **Example**: **Decentraland** and **The Sandbox** allow users to buy virtual land and digital goods with cryptocurrencies like **ETH** and **MANA**. As these virtual currencies grow in popularity, they

168

may face regulatory scrutiny regarding taxation and financial reporting.

- **Intellectual Property Laws**: As mentioned earlier, virtual worlds are home to large amounts of user-generated content, which presents challenges in ensuring that creators' intellectual property is protected. Governments are working to adapt copyright laws to account for digital and virtual assets in the Metaverse.

- **Consumer Protection**: Users in the Metaverse engage in transactions for digital goods, services, and experiences. Protecting consumers from fraud, misrepresentation, and scams is an essential aspect of virtual world regulation. Ensuring that users understand what they are purchasing, especially when it comes to NFTs or virtual property, is crucial for consumer protection.

Conclusion

The legal and ethical considerations in the Metaverse are complex and evolving. Developers must navigate issues related to intellectual property, user rights, privacy, and financial regulation to ensure that their platforms are compliant with laws and that users' rights are respected. As the Metaverse continues to grow, these issues will only become more significant, requiring developers to stay informed and adapt to changing legal landscapes.

Real-world examples like the copyright challenges in **Roblox** and **Fortnite** highlight the importance of clear policies and practices when it comes to user-generated content. Similarly, issues around **data privacy** and **user rights** are becoming increasingly important as more users engage in social, economic, and creative activities in the Metaverse.

In the next chapter, we will explore **governance in the Metaverse**, focusing on the role of community-driven decision-making, decentralized governance models, and the challenges of moderating virtual spaces in a way that respects user rights and fosters positive interactions.

CHAPTER 18

VIRTUAL EVENTS AND EXPERIENCES

Overview: How to Design and Host Virtual Events Like Concerts, Conferences, and Meetups in the Metaverse

Virtual events have become a defining feature of the Metaverse, enabling users to engage in immersive experiences that blend entertainment, education, and social interaction. Whether it's a concert featuring a famous artist, a global conference with experts in various fields, or a casual meetup with friends and colleagues, virtual events provide a unique platform for connecting people in real-time, regardless of their geographical location.

In this chapter, we will explore how to design and host virtual events in the Metaverse, covering everything from concept development and event planning to technical execution and audience engagement. We will look at real-world examples, such as **virtual concerts** in **Fortnite** and virtual festivals on **Roblox** and **Second Life**, to understand what makes these events successful and how developers can create their own memorable virtual experiences.

1. Types of Virtual Events in the Metaverse

Virtual events can take many forms, depending on the purpose, audience, and platform. Some of the most popular types of virtual events include:

- **Concerts and Live Performances**: Virtual concerts are becoming increasingly popular in the Metaverse, offering artists a way to connect with fans in an immersive environment. These concerts often feature live performances with special effects, interactive elements, and virtual meet-and-greets with the artists.
  - **Example**: **Fortnite** has hosted several virtual concerts, including performances by **Travis Scott** and **Marshmello**, attracting millions of players. These concerts featured immersive stages, real-time music, and in-game interactions, allowing players to enjoy the event from the comfort of their homes.
- **Conferences and Panels**: Virtual conferences are an excellent way to gather experts, industry leaders, and enthusiasts in a shared digital space. These events can include keynote speeches, panel discussions, networking opportunities, and exhibitor booths, all hosted in an interactive 3D environment.

- o **Example**: **Second Life** has hosted various virtual conferences, where users can attend seminars, interact with speakers, and engage with fellow attendees. Platforms like **AltspaceVR** and **Mozilla Hubs** are also used to host virtual conferences, offering immersive environments for educational and professional events.

- **Meetups and Social Gatherings**: Virtual meetups offer a more casual experience where users can gather to socialize, share ideas, or collaborate on projects. These events can range from small group chats to large-scale social gatherings in virtual environments.

  - o **Example**: **Roblox** frequently hosts virtual festivals and social events, where players can meet up, play games, and experience live performances together. The platform's open-world nature allows users to create their own events, inviting friends or the entire community to join.

- **Product Launches and Brand Activations**: Companies are increasingly turning to virtual worlds to launch products and host brand activations. These events provide a unique opportunity to engage customers in a highly interactive and visually engaging environment.

- o **Example**: **Gucci** hosted a virtual store opening in **Roblox**, allowing users to explore a virtual fashion boutique, try on virtual items, and purchase limited-edition digital goods. This event helped the brand connect with a younger, tech-savvy audience in the Metaverse.

2. Designing a Virtual Event: Key Considerations

When planning and designing a virtual event in the Metaverse, developers need to consider several important factors to ensure the event is engaging, functional, and accessible for participants.

- **Platform   Selection**: The first step in planning a virtual event is choosing the right platform. Depending on the type of event and the target audience, developers may choose platforms like **Fortnite**, **Roblox**, **Decentraland**, or **VRChat**, each offering unique tools and features for hosting events. It's important to choose a platform that aligns with the event's goals and audience.
  - o **Considerations**:
    - ▪ Is the platform accessible to the intended audience? (e.g., VR access, mobile compatibility)

174

- Does the platform support the type of event you want to host? (e.g., concerts, networking, exhibitions)
- Does the platform offer customization tools to tailor the event environment?

- **Event Structure and Content**: The content and structure of the event will depend on its purpose. For a virtual concert, the event structure will include live performances, visual effects, and crowd interaction. For a conference, the structure may involve keynote speakers, panel discussions, and virtual networking spaces.

  o **Considerations**:
    - How will you create engaging and interactive content?
    - What technologies will you use for live streaming, interactive elements, or VR integration?
    - How will you balance the event's duration and pacing to keep the audience engaged?

- **Interactivity and Engagement**: One of the key advantages of virtual events is the ability to engage the audience in real-time through interactive features. These can include live voting, Q&A sessions, interactive avatars, and mini-games. The more interactive the event, the more likely it is to hold the audience's attention and encourage participation.

- o **Example**: During the. **Travis Scott concert** in **Fortnite**, players could interact with the environment by flying through different dimensions, jumping on platforms, and even controlling their avatars in sync with the music. This level of interaction made the concert an immersive and memorable experience.

- **Social   Features**: Socializing is a key aspect of many virtual events. Allowing users to interact with one another, form groups, and participate in social activities creates a sense of community and enhances the event's experience. Consider adding features like chat rooms, voice communication, or avatars with customizable expressions and animations.

  - o **Considerations**:
    - How will you facilitate social interaction? (e.g., chat rooms, group spaces, private interactions)
    - Will you provide features for networking or making friends within the virtual environment?

3. Real-world Example: Virtual Concerts in Fortnite

Fortnite has become one of the most innovative platforms for hosting virtual events, especially concerts. The in-game concert experience in Fortnite has redefined how players interact with their favorite artists in a virtual setting.

- **Travis Scott's Virtual Concert**: In April 2020, **Travis Scott** held a live virtual concert within **Fortnite**, attracting over 27 million players globally. The event featured a stunning, immersive stage design with surreal visual effects, such as floating islands and a massive version of Travis Scott's avatar interacting with players. Users could navigate the virtual environment while the concert played, offering an interactive, real-time experience unlike anything seen before in traditional gaming.
    - **Key Features of the Event**:
        - **Immersive Environment**: The concert took place on an ever-evolving stage that changed dynamically during the performance.
        - **Real-time Interaction**: Players could jump, dance, and explore different parts of the environment while watching the concert, creating a sense of participation.

177

- **Monetization**: Fortnite also monetized the event through the sale of exclusive in-game items, such as outfits and emotes inspired by Travis Scott.

This event demonstrated the potential of virtual worlds to host large-scale, interactive concerts that appeal to a global audience. It showcased how virtual worlds can be used to bridge the gap between entertainment, gaming, and social interaction.

4. Real-world Example: Virtual Festivals on Roblox and Second Life

In addition to concerts, other types of virtual events like festivals, art exhibitions, and social meetups have become increasingly popular in platforms like **Roblox** and **Second Life**.

- **Virtual Festivals on Roblox**: **Roblox** has hosted several virtual festivals where users can attend live performances, participate in challenges, and engage in themed activities. For example, the **Roblox Egg Hunt** is an annual event where players can explore virtual worlds to find collectible items, while live concerts and special events bring additional interactivity to the experience. These festivals often feature in-game items, themed worlds, and social spaces where players can gather, chat, and experience unique content.

178

- Key Features of the Event:
  - **Gamified Experiences**: Users can complete challenges and quests to earn exclusive items during the festival.
  - **Community Engagement**: Virtual festivals create spaces for social interaction, where players can meet up, participate in games, and share experiences with friends.
- **Virtual Festivals in Second Life**: **Second Life** is another platform that has hosted numerous virtual events, including music festivals, fashion shows, and cultural celebrations. The platform allows creators to build and host events in a fully customizable 3D environment. Users can participate in live performances, explore virtual booths, and interact with other attendees.
  - Key Features of the Event:
    - **Customizable Event Spaces**: Users can design their own venues or attend user-created festivals that feature unique environments and stages.
    - **Monetization Opportunities**: Event hosts and performers can monetize their virtual festivals by selling tickets, merchandise, and special access passes.

5. Best Practices for Hosting Virtual Events

To ensure a successful virtual event, consider the following best practices:

- **Test and Optimize**: Before the event goes live, conduct thorough testing to ensure that all interactive features and technical components function smoothly. Test the event in various conditions and with different user groups to identify potential issues such as server lag or connectivity problems.

- **Promote the Event**: Use social media, in-game messaging, and community forums to promote your event. Build excitement leading up to the event by sharing teasers, behind-the-scenes content, and exclusive previews of what users can expect.

- **Engage the Audience**: During the event, keep the audience engaged by offering interactive elements such as live polls, Q&A sessions, or giveaways. The more immersive and interactive the event, the more likely users are to return for future events.

Conclusion

Virtual events in the Metaverse offer unique opportunities for entertainment, socialization, and business. Whether hosting concerts, festivals, or conferences, developers and creators can leverage virtual worlds to engage audiences in innovative and immersive ways. As demonstrated by real-world examples like **Fortnite's Travis Scott concert** and **Roblox's virtual festivals**, the Metaverse is a powerful platform for connecting people through shared digital experiences.

By considering factors like platform selection, event design, and user engagement, developers can create virtual events that leave a lasting impact. As the Metaverse continues to grow, the possibilities for virtual events will expand, providing even more opportunities for creativity, interaction, and commerce.

In the next chapter, we will explore **the future of virtual events**, discussing emerging trends, technologies, and business models that will shape how we experience events in the Metaverse.

CHAPTER 19

SOCIAL INTERACTIONS IN THE METAVERSE

Overview: The Role of Social Interaction in Virtual Worlds and the Creation of Shared Experiences, Communities, and Networks

Social interaction is at the heart of the Metaverse experience. Just as physical worlds thrive on human connections, virtual worlds are shaped by the relationships, communities, and networks that form within them. The ability to connect with others, form friendships, share experiences, and collaborate across digital environments is what makes virtual worlds so compelling. Whether it's interacting with friends in a game, attending virtual social gatherings, or participating in collaborative workspaces, social interactions drive engagement and foster a sense of belonging in virtual spaces.

In this chapter, we will explore the dynamics of social interaction in the Metaverse, examining how virtual worlds enable users to interact with each other, build relationships, and form communities. We'll look at the various forms of social engagement—ranging from casual meetups to collaborative projects—and explore how platforms like **VRChat** and **Facebook**

Horizon facilitate these interactions. Through real-world examples, we will illustrate the role of socialization in creating vibrant virtual communities and immersive digital experiences.

1. The Role of Social Interaction in Virtual Worlds

In the Metaverse, social interaction is not just a feature—it's the essence of the experience. Socializing in virtual spaces allows users to form connections, share content, collaborate on projects, and participate in shared activities. These interactions are integral to creating engaging, dynamic worlds where users feel like active participants rather than passive consumers.

- **Shared   Experiences**: Virtual worlds offer a way for users to participate in shared experiences, whether it's attending a concert, playing a game, or collaborating on building virtual worlds. These shared experiences create emotional connections between users, even if they are separated by physical distance. The ability to engage with others in real-time and experience something together fosters a sense of community and camaraderie.

- **Virtual   Communities**: Communities are the foundation of social interaction in the Metaverse. These communities can be centered around common interests, activities, or goals, such as gaming clans, virtual art galleries, educational groups, or even virtual workplaces. Social interactions within these communities allow users to bond, share ideas, and collaborate on creative or professional endeavors.

- **User-Generated Content and Social Engagement**: Many virtual worlds encourage **user-generated content (UGC)**, which allows users to create and share their own experiences, assets, and environments. This content-sharing culture fosters social interaction, as users interact with, comment on, and collaborate with each other's creations. The act of sharing and creating together strengthens the sense of community and engagement within virtual worlds.

- **The Metaverse as a Social Space**: Unlike traditional online platforms, the Metaverse is a fully immersive space where users can socialize and interact with one another in ways that go beyond simple text chats or social media posts. Virtual avatars and immersive environments allow for more meaningful interactions, where users can express emotions, body language, and reactions in real-time.

2. Platforms for Social Interaction in the Metaverse

Various platforms in the Metaverse are specifically designed to foster social interaction and enable users to connect with one another. These platforms provide a space for users to meet, socialize, collaborate, and explore virtual worlds together. Let's look at some of the most popular platforms enabling social interactions in the Metaverse:

- **VRChat**:

  VRChat is one of the most well-known platforms for social interaction in the Metaverse. It allows users to create avatars, socialize in virtual worlds, attend events, and play games together. VRChat supports both virtual reality (VR) and non-VR users, providing an accessible space for socializing and interaction. It's a platform where users can connect with others, explore user-generated worlds, and participate in activities like dance parties, concerts, or trivia games. The social dynamics in VRChat are driven by the creativity of the community, with users frequently designing and hosting events for others to attend.

  o **Real-world   Example**:

    In **VRChat**, users often attend virtual hangouts where they socialize with friends, participate in games, or explore new worlds. The platform's avatars, dynamic environments, and interactive features—like voice chat, emotes, and gestures—create a rich social experience. Users can even host their own events, such as virtual meetups, live performances, or themed parties, making VRChat a popular social hub in the Metaverse.

- **Facebook   Horizon**:
Facebook Horizon is another platform designed for social interaction, built by **Meta** (formerly Facebook). Horizon offers a virtual world where users can create avatars, interact with others, explore different worlds, and participate in activities like games, art creation, and collaborative building. It focuses on providing a social experience that mirrors real-life interactions, with users able to communicate, create, and play together in immersive spaces.

  - **Real-world   Example**:
  In **Facebook Horizon**, users can create virtual spaces where they can meet and interact with others. These spaces range from casual hangouts to collaborative environments where users can build, design, and share their creations. Horizon encourages socializing through shared activities such as games, where users can team up with others to solve puzzles, compete, or simply have fun together.

- **Second   Life**:
Second Life has long been a pioneer in creating a virtual world centered around social interaction. With its robust social tools, including chat, voice communication, and

virtual spaces for events, **Second Life** allows users to create and socialize in a fully immersive world. Users can attend virtual concerts, visit art galleries, or participate in business meetings. The platform's emphasis on **user-generated content** fosters a dynamic environment where users continuously interact, create, and engage with each other.

- o **Real-world** **Example**: **Second Life** has hosted various social events, such as virtual weddings, art exhibitions, and music performances. One popular example is the **Second Life Music Festival**, where users gather to listen to live performances by virtual bands and artists. The ability to interact with others in real-time, combined with the platform's vast virtual spaces and customization options, makes it a unique space for socializing in the Metaverse.

3. Socializing in Virtual Worlds: Interaction Tools and Features

The ability to interact and communicate with others is essential to creating a meaningful social experience in the Metaverse. Virtual worlds use a variety of tools and features to enable social engagement and interaction among users.

- **Avatars and Customization**: Avatars serve as a user's representation in virtual worlds, allowing them to interact with others in a visual way. Customizable avatars enable users to express their unique identities, making social interactions more personal and immersive. In many virtual worlds, users can change their avatars' appearance, including clothing, accessories, and even body language, to reflect their personalities.

- **Voice and Text Communication**: Real-time voice and text chat are essential tools for communication in virtual worlds. These tools allow users to talk with each other while exploring, playing games, or attending events. Platforms like **VRChat** and **Second Life** support voice chat, enabling more natural, human-like interactions. Some platforms also support text chat for users who may not have access to voice communication.

- **Emotes and Gestures**: Virtual worlds often include emotes, gestures, and animations that allow users to express emotions and reactions. These features enable users to communicate non-verbally, adding depth and richness to their social interactions. Whether it's waving to a friend, showing excitement with a dance move, or emoting laughter, these tools make social experiences more dynamic and enjoyable.

188

- **Shared   Spaces   and   Events**: Shared spaces like virtual cafes, parks, and game rooms encourage spontaneous social interaction. Virtual events, such as concerts, festivals, and meetups, bring people together for a collective experience. These events foster a sense of community, as participants share common interests and activities.

- **Social   Groups   and   Communities**: Many virtual worlds allow users to join or create social groups based on shared interests or activities. These groups provide a space for members to connect, chat, and collaborate on projects. Some platforms, like **Discord**, have become hubs for virtual world communities, allowing users to organize events, share content, and discuss shared experiences.

4. Real-world Example: Socializing in VRChat

VRChat has become one of the most well-known platforms for social interaction in the Metaverse. The platform allows users to socialize in fully immersive 3D environments, creating a rich, dynamic space for communication and community building.

- **Interactive   Worlds**: In **VRChat**, users can visit a variety of virtual worlds created by other users, ranging from simple chat rooms to highly detailed environments like concert venues, cafes, and gaming spaces. These worlds provide opportunities for socializing, exploring, and participating in shared activities.

- o **Example**: In **VRChat**, players attend virtual concerts, art shows, and trivia nights. Many users also create their own worlds and host social events, such as themed parties, meetups, or game nights. The interactive worlds allow users to engage in a variety of experiences that go beyond traditional gaming.

- **Community   Building**: One of the platform's greatest strengths is its ability to build communities. Users connect based on shared interests, whether they are into gaming, art, fashion, or just socializing. The ability to interact with others through avatars, voice chat, and custom emotes creates a sense of presence and connection that goes beyond simple text or video calls.

---

5. Ethical Considerations in Social Interactions

As virtual worlds continue to grow, ethical considerations related to social interactions are becoming more important. These include:

- **Harassment and Toxic Behavior**: Just as in the real world, virtual spaces can become breeding grounds for harassment, bullying, or toxic behavior. Developers must implement tools for reporting misconduct and moderating interactions to create a safe environment for all users.

- **Privacy and Consent**: Users' personal information and data must be protected in virtual worlds. Ethical concerns arise when it comes to data privacy, consent for interactions, and the collection of user data. Developers must ensure that privacy policies are transparent and that users are aware of how their information is being used.

Conclusion

Social interactions are the foundation of the Metaverse. The ability to meet, collaborate, socialize, and form communities within virtual worlds is what makes these spaces vibrant and engaging. Platforms like **VRChat, Facebook Horizon**, and **Second Life** provide users with the tools to connect, interact, and share experiences in immersive environments. As virtual worlds continue to grow, so too will the opportunities for creating meaningful, dynamic social experiences that span the globe.

In the next chapter, we will dive into **user behavior and ethics in the Metaverse**, exploring how user interactions can shape the virtual world experience, and the challenges of creating a respectful, inclusive community.

CHAPTER 20

BUILDING COMMUNITIES IN VIRTUAL WORLDS

Overview: Strategies for Fostering and Maintaining Healthy, Engaged Communities within Virtual Environments

In the Metaverse, communities are the lifeblood of virtual worlds. These communities are built around shared experiences, common interests, and social interactions that transcend physical locations. For developers, creators, and platform owners, building and nurturing these communities is crucial for the long-term success of their virtual environments. Healthy communities drive engagement, fuel creativity, and create a sense of belonging for users. However, fostering a thriving virtual community requires intentional strategies and continuous effort.

In this chapter, we will explore effective strategies for building and maintaining engaged communities in virtual worlds. From encouraging user-generated content and events to managing social dynamics and inclusivity, we will discuss how to create spaces where users feel valued and invested. We will also explore real-world examples, such as **Second Life** and the rise of **Metaverse influencers**, who play a pivotal role in shaping online communities.

1. The Importance of Community in Virtual Worlds

A thriving virtual community is essential for the success of any Metaverse platform. These communities offer users a sense of **belonging**, provide a space for **social interaction**, and often become self-sustaining ecosystems where users contribute, collaborate, and create.

- **User   Retention**: Community-driven platforms tend to have higher **user retention** rates because users are more likely to return to a space where they have meaningful social interactions. When users feel like they are part of a community, they are more likely to stay engaged and return regularly, even if the content or experience itself doesn't change dramatically.

- **Creative   Collaboration**: Strong communities foster **collaborative creation**. Users often work together to build virtual spaces, create art, develop games, and share knowledge. By encouraging collaboration, virtual worlds can harness the creativity of their communities, leading to innovative content and experiences.

- **User   Empowerment**: When users feel a sense of ownership and influence over their virtual world, they are more likely to contribute.

Community-building efforts that focus on user empowerment help users feel like they are not just passive participants, but active contributors to the virtual environment.

2. Key Strategies for Building and Fostering Communities

Building a successful virtual community requires more than just creating a platform and inviting users. Developers and creators must implement strategies that encourage social interaction, inclusivity, and sustained engagement. Here are some key strategies:

- **Encourage User-Generated Content (UGC)**: User-generated content is the backbone of many virtual worlds. Platforms that allow users to create and share their own content (e.g., avatars, virtual land, art, and games) empower the community to shape the environment and contribute to its growth. UGC not only expands the content available but also fosters a sense of ownership and involvement.
  - o **Example**: **Second Life** allows users to create, buy, and sell virtual goods and spaces. Users can design avatars, create art, build structures, and even host events. This **UGC-driven ecosystem**

helps Second Life remain relevant and keeps the community active and engaged.

- **Host Community Events**: Hosting events is one of the most effective ways to engage your community. These events could be anything from virtual concerts and art shows to gaming tournaments, meetups, and educational sessions. Regularly scheduled events bring users together, encourage socialization, and provide opportunities for new users to connect with the community.

  o **Example**: **Roblox** has become a popular platform for virtual events, with many user-generated games hosting events like **music festivals** or **award shows**. These events allow players to interact in a shared space, enhancing community bonding and engagement.

- **Provide Tools for Collaboration**: Giving users the tools to collaborate on projects— whether it's building a new world, designing a new avatar, or creating a game—helps build a sense of community. When users can work together, they form bonds over shared goals and efforts. Collaboration fosters creativity and allows users to become deeply invested in the virtual world.

  o **Example**: In **Minecraft**, players often collaborate to build massive virtual worlds,

196

castles, or cities. These projects bring players together, and the results of their collective effort become a source of pride and belonging within the community.

- **Implement Effective Moderation**: Community health depends on a safe and respectful environment. Having clear rules, guidelines, and a **moderation team** in place helps ensure that interactions remain positive and productive. Managing toxic behavior, bullying, and harassment is crucial for maintaining a welcoming space for all users.

  - **Example**: **VRChat** has a built-in reporting system that allows users to flag inappropriate behavior, while developers actively moderate spaces to prevent abuse. This ensures that the platform remains a safe and respectful space for users of all backgrounds.

---

3. Community-Driven Content and Events in Second Life

Second Life is a prime example of a platform where **community-driven content** and events have been key to its success. Launched in 2003, Second Life has remained popular for nearly two decades because of its emphasis on user empowerment and social interaction.

- **User-Created Worlds and Content**: In **Second Life**, users are not only able to create their own avatars, but also virtual buildings, landscapes, and entire worlds. This creates an ecosystem of constantly evolving content, with new spaces and activities being created by users every day. The platform's economy is largely driven by these user-created assets, allowing users to buy, sell, and trade goods within the virtual world.

- **Virtual Social Gatherings and Festivals**: Second Life hosts various community-driven events such as virtual concerts, art exhibitions, and fashion shows. These events are organized by both users and developers, often with the participation of virtual brands and artists. **Second Life's Community Events** system helps users find and attend events tailored to their interests, fostering engagement and social interaction.

  o **Example**: The **Second Life Music Festival** is one of the platform's annual highlights, where virtual musicians perform live, and users can interact with the artists. These events help establish Second Life as a dynamic and active platform, with regular social events providing entertainment and opportunities to meet new people.

4. The Rise of Metaverse Influencers

As the Metaverse grows, so does the role of **Metaverse influencers**—individuals who build large followings within virtual worlds. These influencers have become key players in shaping virtual communities and promoting content. Their influence is similar to that of social media influencers, but within the immersive world of virtual environments.

- **Influencers as Community Builders**: Metaverse influencers use their platforms to create and share content, host events, and engage with their audiences. They build strong communities around their personal brands and often collaborate with developers or brands to create exclusive content, experiences, or merchandise for their followers.

- **Branding and Collaboration**: Influencers in the Metaverse often collaborate with virtual world platforms or digital brands to host branded events, product launches, and experiences. These partnerships help bring attention to the platform, attract new users, and increase engagement.
  - o **Example**: Influencers in **Roblox** often collaborate with the platform's developers to create special in-game events, such as limited-edition merchandise drops or virtual concerts. Their followers actively participate in these

events, solidifying their influence in the community.

- **Monetization and Economy**: Just like traditional influencers, Metaverse influencers can monetize their presence through brand deals, virtual merchandise sales, and tips from fans. Many influencers use their influence to sell custom digital assets, such as skins, emotes, or avatars, contributing to the virtual economy.

  o **Example**: On **Twitch**, some streamers host live broadcasts of their in-game experiences in **Fortnite** or **Minecraft**, gaining followers who then participate in the virtual worlds with them. They monetize their presence through donations, sponsorships, and advertising revenue.

5. Best Practices for Community Building in Virtual Worlds

Building and maintaining a thriving virtual community requires ongoing effort and attention. Developers and creators must foster an environment that is welcoming, inclusive, and engaging. Here are some best practices for community building:

- **Encourage Inclusivity and Diversity**: Ensure that your virtual space is welcoming to everyone, regardless of their background, identity, or interests.

200

Provide tools for users to express themselves and be mindful of creating spaces that cater to diverse communities.

- **Recognize and Reward Community Leaders**: Many successful virtual worlds rely on **community leaders**—users who actively engage with others, host events, and create content. Recognizing these leaders and offering them incentives can help foster a sense of ownership and responsibility in the community.

- **Provide Clear Guidelines and Safety Protocols**: It's essential to establish clear community guidelines that define acceptable behavior. Encourage respectful interactions and take action against harassment or toxic behavior. Offering users tools to report violations and protect their privacy is critical to maintaining a safe and supportive community.

- **Maintain Consistent Communication**: Regularly communicate with your community through updates, announcements, and direct interaction. Hosting Q&A sessions or feedback events helps users feel heard and ensures that their concerns are addressed.

Conclusion

Building communities in virtual worlds is a dynamic and ongoing process that requires developers and creators to engage with users, provide meaningful experiences, and foster a sense of belonging. Through **user-generated content**, **community-driven events**, and **social interaction tools**, virtual worlds can become vibrant, thriving spaces where users connect, create, and collaborate.

Real-world examples from **Second Life**, **Roblox**, and the rise of **Metaverse influencers** show how powerful community building can be in virtual spaces. By implementing best practices and continuously evolving the community experience, developers can create virtual worlds that attract, retain, and engage users for years to come.

In the next chapter, we will explore the **ethical challenges of community moderation** in virtual worlds, including issues related to content moderation, user behavior, and the role of developers in managing virtual spaces.

CHAPTER 21

MODERATION AND SAFETY IN THE METAVERSE

Overview: Addressing the Challenges of Moderating User Behavior, Preventing Harassment, and Ensuring Safety in Virtual Worlds

As the Metaverse continues to grow and virtual environments become more immersive, the need for effective moderation and safety measures has never been more critical. In these digital spaces, users from all over the world interact, collaborate, and socialize, often sharing personal experiences, ideas, and creativity. While these environments offer tremendous opportunities for connection, they also present unique challenges when it comes to maintaining a safe, respectful, and inclusive space for all users.

Moderating user behavior, preventing harassment, and ensuring overall safety in the Metaverse require a combination of technological tools, community guidelines, and proactive management. In this chapter, we will explore the importance of moderation in virtual worlds, the strategies used to combat toxic behavior, and how platforms like **VRChat** and **Roblox** enforce community standards to create safer spaces for their users.

1. The Need for Moderation in the Metaverse

Moderation in virtual worlds is essential for several reasons. It ensures that users are interacting in a respectful and secure environment, prevents harmful or inappropriate content from being shared, and fosters a positive experience for all participants.

- **User   Behavior   Management**: In virtual worlds, users can often express themselves freely, which can sometimes lead to the emergence of inappropriate behavior, such as **harassment**, **bullying**, **hate speech**, and **toxicity**. Moderation helps ensure that users are held accountable for their actions and that negative behaviors are addressed swiftly.

- **Content   Moderation**: Virtual worlds often allow users to create and share content, including avatars, text, images, and videos. This can lead to the spread of harmful content, such as explicit material, inappropriate language, or copyrighted works. Effective content moderation systems are necessary to filter and manage what users share within these spaces.

- **Safety   Concerns**: The Metaverse also raises concerns around **user safety**, particularly when it comes to younger users or vulnerable individuals. Cyberbullying, privacy violations, and exposure to harmful or dangerous content can negatively impact users' experiences. Ensuring safety means creating a system that can prevent and mitigate such risks.

- **Building Trust and Community**: When moderation is handled well, it helps build trust among users, as they feel safe and supported within the virtual world. A strong moderation system fosters a healthy, engaged community where users can interact freely and respectfully without fear of harm.

---

2. Types of Moderation in Virtual Worlds

Effective moderation is multi-faceted, involving a combination of technological tools, community guidelines, and human oversight. Here are some of the most common types of moderation systems employed in virtual worlds:

- **Automated Content Moderation**: Automated tools are often used to filter and flag inappropriate content in virtual worlds. These tools scan text, images, videos, and even user interactions for offensive language, explicit content, or hate speech. Advanced algorithms use natural language processing (NLP) to detect harmful words and phrases, while image recognition tools can identify inappropriate visuals.
  - o **Example**: **Roblox** uses automated systems to scan for inappropriate usernames, chat messages,

and in-game content. Any text or images that violate the platform's guidelines are automatically flagged and removed.

- **User   Reporting   Systems**: Most virtual worlds implement user reporting systems that allow players to flag offensive content or inappropriate behavior. These systems are crucial in empowering users to take action when they witness harassment, abuse, or content violations. Reports are typically reviewed by human moderators who can take further action, such as issuing warnings, banning users, or removing content.

  - **Example**: In **VRChat**, users can report toxic behavior, harassment, or inappropriate content through the platform's built-in reporting system. This allows the community to actively contribute to maintaining a safe environment, and reported incidents are reviewed by moderators.

- **Human   Moderators**: While automated systems can catch obvious violations, human moderators play a vital role in ensuring that the platform's rules are followed and that more nuanced issues are addressed. Human moderators review flagged content, investigate reports, and handle disputes between users. They also engage with the community and ensure that the platform's standards are upheld.

- o **Example**: **Second Life** employs both automated tools and human moderators to enforce its community guidelines. The human moderators handle complex cases, such as resolving conflicts between users, managing disputes, and intervening in cases of harassment or abuse.

- **Community Guidelines**: Clear and transparent **community guidelines** are essential for setting expectations around acceptable behavior in virtual worlds. These guidelines outline what is and isn't allowed, providing users with a framework for interaction. By establishing these rules, platforms ensure that users understand the consequences of violating them and encourage a safer, more respectful community.

  - o **Example**: **Roblox** has clear **community standards** that outline prohibited behaviors, including bullying, cheating, and the creation of inappropriate content. These guidelines help users understand what is expected of them and what actions can lead to account suspension or bans.

3. Addressing Toxic Behavior and Harassment

Toxic behavior and harassment are significant challenges in any online community, and virtual worlds are no exception. From bullying and hate speech to sexual harassment and discriminatory actions, these behaviors can significantly harm users' experiences. Platforms must take proactive measures to combat toxicity and create a safe environment for all users.

- **Toxicity in Gaming Communities**: Online gaming communities are often particularly vulnerable to toxic behavior, as competition and anonymity can lead to negative interactions. In the Metaverse, where users spend more time interacting socially and creatively, toxic behavior can be especially damaging. It can drive players away, lower engagement, and create a hostile environment.
  - **Example: VRChat** has become a hotspot for socializing and interaction, but it also faces issues with toxic players. To combat this, the platform employs a combination of automated moderation tools and community-driven reporting to ensure that offensive users are quickly flagged and dealt with. VRChat has also introduced **"safe spaces"** where players can choose to interact only with users who have been verified or reported as non-toxic.
- **Harassment in Virtual Worlds**: Harassment in virtual worlds can take many forms, including verbal abuse, unwanted advances, and even stalking or doxxing (exposing personal information). In

virtual environments where users are deeply immersed in the experience, these incidents can feel particularly invasive and harmful.

- o **Example**: **Roblox** has taken steps to combat harassment by introducing **chat filters** that prevent the use of offensive language, and they have set up a strict policy against harassment. They also provide **parental controls** to help families manage younger users' interactions with others in the game.

- **Creating Safe Spaces**: To combat harassment and toxicity, developers are increasingly creating "safe spaces" where users can socialize without fear of being harassed or exposed to inappropriate content. These safe spaces are often accessible through filters or settings that allow users to limit who can interact with them.

  - o **Example**: In **VRChat**, players can **block** or **mute** users they don't want to interact with, effectively removing harmful individuals from their experience. Additionally, the platform provides customizable **avatar settings** to ensure that players can control their level of exposure to potentially harmful interactions.

4. Privacy and Data Protection in the Metaverse

As users increasingly share personal information in virtual worlds—whether it's through avatars, social interactions, or transactions—privacy and data protection become critical considerations. Developers must ensure that user data is protected, personal information is kept private, and users have control over what they share.

- **Data Privacy Laws**: Different countries have varying laws regarding data privacy, and these laws apply to virtual worlds as well. Platforms that operate globally must comply with **privacy regulations** such as the **General Data Protection Regulation (GDPR)** in the European Union, which ensures that users' personal information is protected.
  - o **Example**: **Second Life** and other platforms have updated their privacy policies and data handling practices to ensure they comply with GDPR and other data protection laws. Users are often given the option to control their privacy settings, including who can access their personal information and interactions.
- **User Control Over Data**: Users must have control over their personal data and who can access it. Platforms that respect users' privacy and

provide them with control over their data will foster trust and loyalty.

- o **Example**: **Facebook Horizon** and other Metaverse platforms allow users to manage their privacy settings, such as choosing who can see their profile or interact with them, making it easier for users to have control over their data and interactions.

5. Best Practices for Moderation and Safety in Virtual Worlds

To create and maintain a safe environment in virtual worlds, developers and creators should implement a range of strategies that combine technological solutions with community engagement.

- **Establish Clear Community Guidelines**: Clear and accessible community guidelines help set expectations for behavior and provide users with a framework for acceptable conduct. These guidelines should be easy to understand and regularly updated to reflect evolving community needs.
- **Implement Comprehensive Reporting Systems**: Users should be empowered to report inappropriate behavior or content easily. A transparent and efficient

reporting system helps ensure that users feel supported and protected when incidents occur.

- **Create Safe Spaces**: Offer users the ability to control their interactions by providing tools like mute, block, and safe zones. These tools allow users to protect themselves from harmful interactions, fostering a more positive experience.

- **Regularly Update Moderation Tools**: As virtual worlds grow, the need for more advanced moderation tools increases. Developers should continually update their automated moderation systems, ensuring they can detect and prevent new forms of harmful behavior.

- **Promote Inclusivity and Respect**: Encourage respectful behavior and inclusivity within the community. Create spaces where diverse voices are valued, and promote a culture of kindness and collaboration.

Conclusion

Moderation and safety are essential components of any virtual world, especially as the Metaverse becomes an increasingly popular space for socializing, gaming, and creating. Developers must implement robust moderation systems, enforce community guidelines, and protect user privacy to ensure a safe and welcoming environment. By addressing issues of harassment, toxicity, and data privacy, developers can foster healthy communities where users can interact and collaborate freely.

Real-world examples from platforms like **VRChat** and **Roblox** show how effective moderation and safety measures can protect users while maintaining an engaging, dynamic space for interaction. As virtual worlds continue to evolve, the responsibility to safeguard users' experiences will remain a critical focus, ensuring that the Metaverse remains a place where everyone can feel safe, respected, and valued.

In the next chapter, we will explore the **future of Metaverse moderation**, examining emerging technologies, trends, and the evolving role of AI and automation in creating safer virtual environments.

CHAPTER 22

THE FUTURE OF VIRTUAL REALITY AND AUGMENTED REALITY

Overview: The Ongoing Evolution of VR and AR Technology and How They Will Shape the Future of the Metaverse

The Metaverse is not a single, static concept; it is a rapidly evolving digital space that blends virtual reality (VR), augmented reality (AR), and other cutting-edge technologies. At the forefront of this evolution are **VR** and **AR**, two technologies that are transforming how we interact with the digital world and each other. These technologies are becoming increasingly sophisticated, offering new ways to experience, socialize, work, and play in immersive environments. As VR and AR continue to advance, they will play a pivotal role in shaping the Metaverse, enabling richer, more realistic, and engaging experiences.

In this chapter, we will explore the future of **Virtual Reality (VR)** and **Augmented Reality (AR)**, examining how these technologies are evolving and how they will contribute to the growth of the Metaverse. We will also look at real-world examples, such as **Facebook's Oculus VR** push and the success of **Pokémon Go** as an AR application, to understand how VR and AR are already shaping virtual and augmented environments today.

1. The Evolution of Virtual Reality (VR)

Virtual Reality (VR) refers to the use of immersive, computer-generated environments in which users can interact as though they are physically present in that environment. VR typically requires specialized hardware, such as **headsets**, **controllers**, and **motion sensors**, to provide an interactive experience.

- **The Early Stages of VR**: VR technology has come a long way from its early days in the 1990s. Initially, VR was largely a niche technology used for gaming and simulations. The headsets were bulky, the graphics were rudimentary, and the overall experience was limited. Despite this, VR had the potential to transport users to entirely new digital worlds, and that potential was evident even in its early iterations.

- **The Modern VR Revolution**: Over the past decade, VR technology has experienced significant advancements, driven by powerful hardware improvements and innovations in software development. **Oculus VR**, now owned by **Meta (formerly Facebook)**, has been one of the most influential players in the VR market, making the technology more accessible to the

215

general public. Devices like the **Oculus Rift, Oculus Quest**, and **Oculus Quest 2** offer wireless, high-quality VR experiences that don't require a high-end gaming PC, making VR more mainstream.

- **Immersive   Experiences**: Modern VR systems use advanced motion tracking, high-definition displays, and spatial audio to create highly immersive environments. Users can walk, move, and interact within 3D spaces, whether for gaming, socializing, learning, or exploring virtual worlds.

- **The   Future   of   VR**: As VR technology continues to improve, we can expect even more immersive and interactive experiences. Future VR headsets will likely become lighter, more comfortable, and more portable, with enhanced graphics and improved haptic feedback systems that simulate touch. VR will also see wider applications in various industries, including education, healthcare, and remote work.

    o   **Example**: **Meta's push into the Metaverse** with the **Oculus Quest 2** and the development of **Horizon Worlds** is a prime example of how VR is advancing. Meta's Metaverse vision aims to create a fully immersive social space where users can interact, work, and socialize using VR headsets, signaling a shift toward a more connected, virtual world.

---

2. The Evolution of Augmented Reality (AR)

Augmented Reality (AR) overlays digital content onto the real world, blending virtual elements with the user's physical environment. Unlike VR, which immerses users in a completely digital world, AR enhances the real world by superimposing interactive digital elements onto it, which can be seen through devices like **smartphones**, **AR glasses**, or **headsets**.

- **The   Rise   of   AR**:
  AR has gained tremendous popularity in recent years, with applications spanning various industries. The most well-known early example of AR is **Pokémon Go**, a mobile game that became a global phenomenon by allowing users to catch virtual Pokémon in the real world through their smartphones. AR technology uses the phone's camera and sensors to place digital objects in real-world environments, giving users the experience of seeing virtual elements in their surroundings.

- **AR's   Growing   Impact**:
  Beyond gaming, AR is increasingly being used for practical applications such as navigation, education, and shopping. **IKEA**, for example, has an AR app that allows

users to visualize how furniture will look in their homes before making a purchase. In the medical field, AR is being used for surgical planning and education, helping doctors visualize complex procedures.

- **The Future of AR**: As AR technology continues to evolve, we can expect it to become more seamless, integrated into everyday life, and more immersive. The development of **AR glasses** and **contact lenses** will allow users to experience AR without the need for a smartphone or bulky headset, creating a more natural and hands-free experience. Additionally, AR's integration with AI and 5G networks will enable real-time, context-aware interactions that will further blur the line between the physical and digital worlds.

  - **Example**: **Pokémon Go** remains one of the most successful AR applications, demonstrating the potential for blending gaming with real-world interaction. The game's popularity continues to thrive, with Niantic, the game's developer, expanding its AR technology to other applications, including **Harry Potter: Wizards Unite** and **Ingress Prime**.

3. How VR and AR Will Shape the Future of the Metaverse

Both VR and AR technologies will play a critical role in shaping the future of the Metaverse, which aims to be a fully immersive, interconnected virtual world where users can socialize, work, create, and play. Here's how VR and AR will drive the next generation of Metaverse experiences:

- **Full Immersion in Virtual Environments** (VR): VR technology will provide the backbone for fully immersive Metaverse experiences, enabling users to enter and interact within 3D environments that feel real. This will allow people to attend virtual meetings, explore digital spaces, participate in social events, and even work in virtual offices. VR headsets, like the **Oculus Quest**, will continue to evolve, providing more lifelike experiences with greater comfort and mobility.
  - o **Example**: Meta's **Horizon Workrooms** is a virtual office space where users can meet, collaborate, and share ideas in a 3D virtual environment using Oculus VR headsets. As VR technology improves, these virtual workspaces will become more sophisticated, making remote work feel more natural and collaborative.
- **Blending the Physical and Virtual Worlds** (AR): AR will play a crucial role in creating **hybrid experiences** in the Metaverse. It will allow users to access virtual

information while still being aware of and interacting with the physical world around them. For instance, AR glasses could display digital content, such as virtual objects or holograms, overlaid on real-world objects. This will enable users to experience both worlds simultaneously, enhancing productivity, gaming, and social interaction.

- o **Example**: **Apple's AR glasses** (rumored to be released in the coming years) are expected to revolutionize how we interact with digital content in the real world. These glasses could integrate with the Metaverse, allowing users to interact with virtual objects while going about their daily activities, from navigating a city to interacting with virtual advertisements or gaming experiences.

- **Increased Interactivity and Personalization**: The combination of VR and AR will enable users to create highly interactive and personalized virtual experiences. From customizing avatars and environments to engaging in real-time social interactions, VR and AR will allow for more dynamic, responsive, and tailored experiences that adapt to each user's preferences and actions.

  - o **Example**: **AR-powered experiences** in **retail** could allow customers to virtually try on clothes or visualize furniture in their homes before making a purchase. Meanwhile, VR experiences

220

could offer personalized virtual tours of distant locations or unique events, providing users with fully customizable travel, entertainment, and shopping experiences in the Metaverse.

---

4. Challenges and Opportunities Ahead for VR and AR in the Metaverse

As VR and AR continue to evolve, they face both challenges and opportunities that will shape their role in the future of the Metaverse.

- **Challenges**:
    - o **Hardware Limitations**: While VR and AR technologies have advanced significantly, there are still limitations in terms of hardware size, weight, and affordability. For example, VR headsets can be cumbersome, and AR glasses are still in the early stages of development. For the Metaverse to reach its full potential, these hardware challenges need to be addressed.
    - o **Social Acceptance**: As VR and AR technologies become more mainstream, there may be challenges in terms of how comfortable users are with spending long periods in immersive environments. Overcoming concerns about

physical strain, mental health, and social isolation will be key to the widespread adoption of these technologies.

- o **Privacy and Security**: The use of VR and AR in the Metaverse raises concerns about data privacy and user security. As these technologies collect data about users' physical movements, interactions, and environments, it will be crucial to develop safeguards to protect users' privacy.

- **Opportunities**:
  - o **Immersive Education and Training**: VR and AR will revolutionize education by providing immersive learning experiences. Whether it's virtual field trips, interactive anatomy lessons, or remote collaboration in science labs, these technologies will provide unprecedented opportunities for learning and skill-building.
  - o **Virtual Socializing and Work**: The Metaverse will provide opportunities for people to work and socialize remotely in ways that feel more natural and engaging than traditional video calls or text chats. Virtual workspaces and social hubs will bridge the gap between physical and digital worlds, allowing for seamless collaboration and socialization.

Conclusion

The future of the Metaverse will be heavily influenced by advancements in **Virtual Reality (VR)** and **Augmented Reality (AR)**. These technologies will make virtual environments more immersive, interactive, and accessible, allowing users to engage with each other and their surroundings in new and exciting ways. With platforms like **Oculus VR** and applications like **Pokémon Go**, VR and AR are already proving their potential, and as these technologies continue to evolve, the Metaverse will become an increasingly integral part of our digital lives.

The ongoing development of VR and AR will provide endless opportunities for innovation, education, work, and social interaction in the Metaverse. By overcoming current challenges and embracing the opportunities that these technologies present, the Metaverse will offer users an even more immersive and interconnected world, transforming how we work, play, and communicate.

In the next chapter, we will delve into the **future of digital currencies and blockchain** in the Metaverse, exploring how decentralized technologies will shape the economy and governance of virtual worlds.

CHAPTER 23

ARTIFICIAL INTELLIGENCE IN THE METAVERSE

Overview: How AI is Being Used to Enhance User Experiences, Create Intelligent NPCs (Non-Playable Characters), and Improve Content Creation in Virtual Worlds

Artificial Intelligence (AI) is becoming a cornerstone of the Metaverse, with its potential to revolutionize virtual worlds by enhancing user experiences, improving content creation, and introducing intelligent non-playable characters (NPCs) that interact with users in more lifelike and dynamic ways. AI-driven elements bring greater immersion, interactivity, and personal engagement to virtual environments, making them more responsive, adaptive, and enjoyable for users.

From NPCs that simulate realistic human behavior to tools that automatically generate environments, AI is helping developers create more dynamic and expansive virtual worlds. In this chapter, we'll explore how AI is being used in the Metaverse to enrich the virtual experience, create smarter NPCs, and streamline content creation. We'll also look at real-world examples of AI

224

applications in virtual worlds, such as AI-driven characters in **The Sims** or **virtual assistants** in customer service scenarios.

1. The Role of AI in Enhancing User Experiences

In the Metaverse, user experience (UX) is paramount. AI technologies can be leveraged to ensure users have smoother, more personalized, and immersive experiences. AI plays a crucial role in adapting the virtual environment to the needs and preferences of individual users, as well as making interactions more engaging and intuitive.

- **Personalization**:
  One of the most powerful uses of AI in the Metaverse is its ability to personalize experiences for each user. AI can track user preferences, behaviors, and interactions within the virtual world and adapt the environment accordingly. This personalization can extend to avatars, content recommendations, and even the storyline of a virtual world.
  - o **Example**: In **The Sims**, AI is used to simulate complex character behaviors and personalize experiences based on the player's actions. Sims' behavior is influenced by AI algorithms that take into account the player's choices, creating unique

and evolving narratives based on those interactions.

- **Adaptive** **Environments**: AI can enable virtual worlds to evolve in real-time based on the actions and decisions of users. For example, dynamic weather systems, day/night cycles, and environmental changes can all be driven by AI, making the virtual world feel more alive and responsive.

  o **Example**: In **Minecraft**, AI-powered mods can create evolving worlds that change according to the player's activities. For example, NPCs in the world may adapt to the player's actions, or environmental changes like storms and seasons may occur based on the player's progress.

- **Intelligent NPCs (Non-Playable Characters)**: AI is central to creating intelligent NPCs that are not just passive, scripted entities, but active participants in the game or virtual world. These NPCs can engage in realistic conversations, adapt to user behavior, and provide dynamic quests and challenges. AI allows these characters to react naturally to different situations and user inputs, providing a more engaging and interactive experience.

2. AI-Driven NPCs in the Metaverse

Non-playable characters (NPCs) are key elements in many virtual worlds, games, and simulations. While traditional NPCs often follow pre-scripted behaviors, AI is now making it possible for these characters to think, learn, and respond in a more intelligent, human-like manner. AI-driven NPCs can enhance immersion, provide challenges, and serve as helpful assistants within virtual worlds.

- **Behavioral AI in NPCs**: AI enables NPCs to exhibit more complex and varied behaviors, such as learning from player interactions, reacting to player decisions, and even evolving over time. NPCs with AI can simulate emotions, preferences, and goals that align with the narrative or gameplay.
  - **Example**: In **The Sims**, AI determines how each Sim interacts with their environment, other Sims, and the player. Sims can autonomously carry out tasks, form relationships, and react to the player's choices in a way that feels lifelike and unique to each interaction.
- **AI in Quest and Narrative Design**: AI can also drive the creation of dynamic narratives and quests in virtual worlds. NPCs can generate storylines that are tailored to the player's actions and decisions, making each player's journey feel unique. Instead of following

static, predetermined scripts, AI-powered NPCs can offer a more interactive and personalized experience.

- o **Example**: In role-playing games (RPGs) like **The Elder Scrolls V: Skyrim**, NPCs are designed with complex dialogue systems powered by AI. These NPCs react to the player's choices and provide different responses based on their own in-game relationships and motivations. As a result, players can have diverse experiences depending on how they engage with NPCs and the world.

- **AI and Player Interactions**: AI can enhance the way players interact with NPCs. Natural Language Processing (NLP) is increasingly being integrated into virtual worlds, allowing players to engage in realistic, free-form conversations with AI-driven NPCs. These interactions can range from simple chats to complex problem-solving scenarios.

  - o **Example**: In **AI Dungeon**, an interactive text-based adventure game powered by OpenAI's GPT-3 model, the AI dynamically generates stories based on the user's inputs. Players can interact with NPCs in natural language, and the game responds in real-time with unique story elements and challenges.

228

3. AI in Content Creation for Virtual Worlds

Beyond enhancing user interactions, AI is also playing a significant role in **content creation** for virtual worlds. As virtual environments become larger and more complex, AI tools can assist developers in creating content faster, more efficiently, and with greater variety. These tools are revolutionizing the way developers build environments, characters, and stories, making the process more accessible and scalable.

- **Procedural Content Generation (PCG)**: AI can automate the creation of vast, procedurally generated content in virtual worlds. **Procedural generation** allows developers to create expansive worlds without manually crafting every element, enabling more dynamic and varied environments. AI-driven systems can generate landscapes, cities, dungeons, and other in-game assets based on predefined parameters, giving players new experiences with every visit.
  - Example: In **Minecraft**, the world is procedurally generated, with AI algorithms creating unique terrains, biomes, and resources for each new world. This ensures that no two experiences are the same, enhancing replayability and player engagement.
- **AI-Generated Art and Environments**: AI can also assist with **art generation**, creating textures,

landscapes, and even entire virtual environments. Tools like **DeepArt** and **Artbreeder** use machine learning to generate visually stunning art based on user input. In the Metaverse, these tools can automate the process of creating environments, making it easier for developers to design large-scale, complex worlds.

- o **Example**: In **The Sandbox**, a decentralized virtual world, creators can use AI-driven tools to design digital assets, like buildings or avatars, without requiring advanced technical skills. These tools make it possible for non-technical users to create virtual goods and environments, expanding the creativity and diversity of content in the Metaverse.

- **AI-Assisted Storytelling**: AI can also assist developers in creating branching narratives, interactive storylines, and personalized experiences for users. By analyzing player behavior and decision-making, AI can tailor the story to fit each player's unique journey.

  - o **Example**: In **AI Dungeon**, players use natural language input to shape the narrative, while AI continuously adapts the story in real-time based on player choices. This creates an infinite variety of stories, making the experience feel unique for every player.

4. Real-world Example: AI-driven Characters in The Sims

The Sims is a prime example of how AI can be used to create intelligent, reactive NPCs that add depth and complexity to virtual worlds. The game uses AI to simulate a wide range of behaviors, from basic interactions to complex relationships and emotional states.

- **AI-Driven   Behavior**:
  In **The Sims**, AI controls the actions of each Sim, determining how they interact with others, how they respond to their environment, and how they pursue their goals. The AI takes into account numerous factors, such as the Sim's personality, needs, and preferences, which influence their behavior and decisions.
  - o **Example**: A Sim might autonomously cook dinner if they are hungry, greet other Sims when they enter the room, or engage in a conversation if they are feeling social. Over time, the AI adapts based on the player's choices, creating a unique experience for each Sim and household.
- **Emotion   Simulation**:
  The Sims AI also simulates emotions, with Sims reacting to events based on their mood and emotional state. This emotional simulation makes the characters feel more lifelike and responsive to the player's actions.

- o **Example**: If a Sim's partner dies, the Sim's mood will dramatically change, and they may exhibit signs of sadness or grief. These emotional responses, powered by AI, make the virtual world feel more alive and dynamic.

---

5. The Future of AI in the Metaverse

The role of AI in the Metaverse is still in its early stages, but as AI technologies continue to advance, we can expect even more sophisticated and lifelike experiences. Here are some potential future developments for AI in virtual worlds:

- **Smarter NPCs**: AI-powered NPCs will continue to evolve, becoming more human-like in their behavior and interactions. They may possess their own desires, motivations, and story arcs, contributing to more dynamic and interactive storytelling.

- **Enhanced Personalization**: AI will enable even greater levels of **personalization** in the Metaverse, tailoring experiences, environments, and interactions to each user's preferences. Players might have their own unique AI companions or virtual assistants that adapt to their gameplay style.

- **AI as Content Creators**: AI may eventually play a more active role in **content creation**, autonomously designing virtual spaces, characters, and art based on user input. This could democratize content creation, allowing anyone to build and contribute to virtual worlds without advanced technical skills.

- **AI-Enhanced Social Interactions**: As AI continues to improve, it will enable more realistic and meaningful social interactions in virtual worlds. AI may serve as social facilitators, mediating conversations, helping users navigate virtual environments, or even recommending events or activities based on user preferences.

Conclusion

AI is rapidly becoming a vital tool in the development of the Metaverse, enhancing user experiences, creating intelligent NPCs, and streamlining content creation. As VR and AR technologies continue to evolve, AI will play an even larger role in making virtual worlds more immersive, dynamic, and personalized. Real-world examples from **The Sims**, **Pokémon Go**, and **AI Dungeon** illustrate the immense potential of AI to transform virtual environments and improve how users interact with them.

Looking ahead, AI will continue to push the boundaries of what is possible in the Metaverse, from intelligent, self-learning characters to autonomous content generation. As AI technologies advance, we can expect virtual worlds to become increasingly responsive and interactive, offering users deeper, more meaningful experiences.

In the next chapter, we will explore **AI-driven virtual economies**, focusing on how AI can influence digital asset creation, transactions, and the overall economy within the Metaverse.

CHAPTER 24

CROSS-PLATFORM
INTEGRATION

Overview: The Future of Interoperability and Cross-Platform Experiences in the Metaverse, Where Users Can Move Seamlessly Between Different Virtual Worlds

The Metaverse is envisioned as a vast, interconnected digital universe—a space where users can move seamlessly between different virtual worlds, platforms, and experiences. One of the key challenges in creating this expansive digital realm is ensuring **interoperability**—the ability for virtual worlds and applications to communicate, share data, and allow users to transition smoothly between them. Cross-platform integration is essential for building a Metaverse that is inclusive, accessible, and enjoyable for everyone, regardless of the device they use or the platform they interact with.

In this chapter, we will explore the importance of cross-platform integration in the Metaverse and the role it plays in creating a unified experience. We will discuss the future of interoperability, how different platforms and virtual worlds can work together, and the technical and business challenges involved. We will also highlight real-world examples, such as **cross-platform play** in

Fortnite and the integration of **VR/AR apps** across multiple devices, to show how these concepts are already shaping the future of the Metaverse.

1. Understanding Cross-Platform Integration in the Metaverse

Cross-platform integration refers to the ability for users to access and interact with virtual worlds, games, and experiences across multiple devices and platforms. This could involve players using different hardware—such as VR headsets, desktops, smartphones, or gaming consoles—and still having the ability to participate in the same experiences, share content, or interact with other users in real-time.

The goal of cross-platform integration in the Metaverse is to break down the barriers between different virtual environments, creating a seamless and interoperable experience. Whether users are on a high-end gaming PC, a mobile device, or a VR headset, they should be able to interact with the same virtual world, access the same content, and communicate with each other without any disruption.

- **Platform   Agnosticism**:
  In the Metaverse, platforms must be agnostic, meaning that they do not favor one specific device or software. The experience should be consistent across various devices

and systems, providing an equitable user experience regardless of how a user accesses the virtual world.

- **Data Sharing and Compatibility**: For true interoperability, platforms must be able to share data seamlessly. This means that user accounts, content, and interactions should be compatible across different platforms. A user's progress, assets, and social connections in one virtual world should be accessible when they transition to another.

- **Unified Identity and Assets**: A key component of cross-platform integration is the ability to maintain a unified digital identity and assets across different virtual environments. Users should be able to move between platforms with their avatars, virtual goods, and achievements intact. This would enable a truly **interoperable Metaverse**, where a user's virtual presence is consistent across all spaces.

2. Real-world Example: Cross-Platform Play in Fortnite

Fortnite has become a trailblazer in terms of cross-platform play and integration, allowing players from different devices—such as **PlayStation**, **Xbox**, **PC**, **Nintendo Switch**, and **mobile**—to play together in the same game world. This has not only expanded the reach of Fortnite but also set a precedent for how cross-platform gaming can work in the Metaverse.

- **Seamless Gameplay Across Platforms**: Fortnite's success lies in its ability to allow players to join the same matches regardless of the platform they're using. Whether a player is using a console, PC, or mobile phone, they can compete in the same game world, interact with others, and experience the same gameplay mechanics.

  o **Example**: A **Fortnite** player on **PlayStation** can team up with friends who are playing on **Xbox** or **PC**. The game synchronizes progress, leaderboards, and rewards across all platforms, allowing players to maintain their achievements no matter where they log in from.

- **Business Model and Accessibility**: By enabling cross-platform play, Fortnite has also made the game more accessible, drawing a larger and more diverse audience. Players aren't restricted by hardware choices, and they can continue playing with their friends even if they own different gaming consoles or devices.

- **Impact on the Metaverse**: Fortnite's cross-platform success demonstrates the power of seamless integration in virtual spaces. As the Metaverse continues to evolve, cross-platform play will be a critical feature that allows users to interact with each other in a shared space, regardless of their device or platform.

3. The Integration of VR/AR Apps Across Multiple Devices

As **Virtual Reality (VR)** and **Augmented Reality (AR)** technologies continue to grow, the demand for cross-platform integration in these spaces becomes more pronounced. Users will want to access AR and VR experiences from various devices—VR headsets, smartphones, AR glasses, and even desktops—and still have a consistent, immersive experience.

- **VR/AR Interoperability**: Currently, VR and AR experiences are often limited by device compatibility, meaning that a VR experience on an Oculus headset may not be accessible on a PlayStation VR or a mobile device. However, future Metaverse platforms will need to address this issue by ensuring that VR and AR apps can function seamlessly across different devices, enabling users to transition between experiences with ease.

- **Cross-Device Content Sharing**: VR and AR apps in the Metaverse will need to allow users to share content between platforms. For example, a user who creates a 3D model of a virtual object in VR could share it with a friend who is viewing the model via an AR application on their phone. This will require real-time synchronization and seamless integration between platforms.

o **Example**: **Pokémon Go**, one of the most successful AR apps, allows users to experience the game both in augmented reality on smartphones and through **AR glasses**. This type of integration is just the beginning of the cross-platform future, where users will be able to move between different AR/VR experiences and still enjoy a cohesive, connected experience.

- **Unified AR/VR Platforms**: Platforms like **Meta's Horizon Worlds** are working toward building a unified experience where users can interact with the Metaverse through both VR and AR devices. This means that whether a user is wearing a VR headset or using an AR app on their phone, they will be able to access the same virtual environments, meet other users, and share experiences.

4. The Technical Challenges of Cross-Platform Integration

Building a seamless cross-platform experience in the Metaverse is not without its challenges. Several technical issues must be addressed to ensure smooth interoperability across different virtual worlds and devices.

- **Standardization**:
  One of the biggest hurdles to cross-platform integration is

the lack of standardization across devices, platforms, and virtual worlds. For the Metaverse to function seamlessly, industry standards need to be established for things like avatars, virtual assets, and even environmental design. Without a common set of rules and protocols, users may find it difficult to move between platforms or carry their virtual identities and assets with them.

- **Data Synchronization**: Synchronizing data across platforms is another major challenge. User progress, virtual goods, and even social interactions must be tracked and updated in real-time across all devices. Achieving this level of integration requires sophisticated cloud-based systems, powerful servers, and low-latency networks to ensure a smooth experience for users.

- **Security and Privacy**: As users move across different platforms in the Metaverse, maintaining security and privacy becomes increasingly complex. Developers must ensure that personal data, transaction histories, and user-generated content are protected across multiple devices and platforms. Cross-platform data sharing also raises concerns about data privacy and the potential for breaches, which must be addressed through robust security measures.

5. Real-world Example: The Integration of VR/AR Apps on Various Devices

The integration of VR/AR apps across different devices is already beginning to take shape, and the success of apps like **Pokémon Go** and **Meta's Horizon Worlds** serves as a proof of concept for the potential of cross-platform experiences.

- **Pokémon   Go**:
  Launched in 2016, **Pokémon Go** remains one of the most successful AR apps in the world. The game allows players to use their smartphones to find and capture virtual Pokémon in the real world. The game's success lies in its ability to provide a consistent experience across multiple devices, with seamless synchronization between players' progress and achievements. Niantic, the game's developer, is continuing to expand the AR features of the app, with future plans to integrate additional devices, such as AR glasses.

- **Meta's   Horizon   Worlds**:
  Meta is positioning itself as a leader in the Metaverse with its **Horizon Worlds**, a virtual space designed for social interaction, creation, and entertainment. Horizon Worlds supports cross-platform play, meaning that users can engage with the same virtual environment whether they are using a **Meta Quest VR headset**, a **PC**, or even AR devices in the future. This integration across devices

ensures a more accessible and unified experience for users.

6. The Future of Cross-Platform Integration in the Metaverse

The future of the Metaverse lies in its ability to offer a truly **interoperable and cross-platform experience**. As more devices, platforms, and virtual worlds come online, cross-platform integration will become a critical component in the development of a unified Metaverse.

- **Universal Avatars and Digital Identity**: One of the next steps in cross-platform integration is the creation of **universal avatars** and digital identities that can seamlessly move between different virtual worlds. Whether you're playing a game, attending a virtual concert, or working in a virtual office, your avatar should represent you consistently across all platforms.

- **Cross-World Interactions**: In the future, users will be able to interact across different virtual worlds in a more unified manner. Imagine attending a virtual conference in one Metaverse world, then hopping over to another world to join a gaming session or attend a live concert—without losing any of your data or digital identity in the process.

243

- **Decentralized Interoperability**: Blockchain and decentralized technologies could play a major role in facilitating cross-platform interoperability. By using decentralized platforms and NFTs

CHAPTER 25

THE BUSINESS OF THE METAVERSE

Overview: The Growing Business Opportunities in the Metaverse, from Real Estate to Virtual Commerce

The Metaverse is rapidly transforming from a futuristic concept into a lucrative business ecosystem, offering numerous opportunities across various industries. As virtual worlds become more immersive and interconnected, the business potential of the Metaverse continues to expand. From virtual real estate and digital fashion to virtual commerce and services, the Metaverse is paving the way for new business models, revenue streams, and entrepreneurial ventures.

In this chapter, we will explore the growing business opportunities within the Metaverse. We'll look at how virtual land, digital assets, and virtual services are being monetized, and discuss the rise of Metaverse-related startups. We will also delve into real-world examples, such as the **purchase of virtual land in Decentraland** and the burgeoning industry of **virtual goods and services** that have already begun to make waves in the digital economy.

1. Virtual Real Estate: A New Frontier for Investment

One of the most intriguing and rapidly developing sectors in the Metaverse is **virtual real estate**. Just like in the physical world, virtual real estate involves the buying, selling, and leasing of digital land and property within virtual worlds. However, virtual real estate offers unique opportunities for businesses, developers, and investors looking to establish a presence in the Metaverse.

- **The Value of Virtual Land**: Virtual real estate can include plots of land, buildings, and entire environments in Metaverse platforms such as **Decentraland**, **The Sandbox**, **Somnium Space**, and **Cryptovoxels**. These platforms allow users to buy and develop digital spaces, which can be used for various purposes such as creating virtual storefronts, hosting events, or even building virtual cities. The value of virtual land is driven by demand, scarcity, and the potential for future development.

  - **Example**: In **Decentraland**, a popular virtual world, parcels of land are bought and sold as NFTs (Non-Fungible Tokens). Some virtual plots in Decentraland have sold for hundreds of thousands of dollars. These properties can be used to build virtual storefronts, art galleries, or entertainment venues, and the value of these properties has increased as more users and businesses enter the Metaverse.

- **Investment and Development**: Investors are increasingly purchasing virtual land as a long-term asset, with the expectation that the value of these digital spaces will increase over time. Developers, on the other hand, are creating virtual environments and experiences that generate revenue through digital commerce, advertising, and other virtual services. These virtual properties can also be leased or rented out for events, advertising space, or other commercial ventures.

  o **Example**: In 2021, **Tokens.com**, a firm focused on virtual real estate investments, purchased a virtual plot in Decentraland for $2.4 million. This plot of land is intended to host virtual fashion shows, luxury events, and entertainment experiences, capitalizing on the growing demand for digital luxury.

---

2. Virtual Goods and Digital Commerce

Another significant business opportunity in the Metaverse lies in **virtual goods** and **digital commerce**. Virtual items, from avatars and skins to accessories, collectibles, and digital assets, are becoming an integral part of the Metaverse economy. These digital goods are bought and sold within virtual worlds using cryptocurrencies or platform-specific tokens.

- **Virtual   Goods**:
  In the Metaverse, users can purchase virtual goods to enhance their experience or showcase their identity. This can include custom clothing for avatars, virtual accessories, land, and even digital art. These virtual goods often have intrinsic value within the Metaverse and can sometimes be resold or traded for profit.
    - **Example**: In **Fortnite**, virtual goods such as skins, emotes, and battle passes have generated billions of dollars in revenue. Players purchase these items using **V-bucks**, the in-game currency, to customize their avatars or unlock exclusive content. Fortnite's success in digital commerce highlights the potential for virtual goods to drive revenue in the Metaverse.
- **The   Rise   of   NFTs**:
  Non-Fungible Tokens (NFTs) are rapidly becoming a key component of the Metaverse's digital economy. NFTs are unique digital assets that are stored on a blockchain, ensuring their rarity and ownership. These tokens are used to represent virtual goods such as digital art, in-game items, and even virtual real estate.
    - **Example**: In **The Sandbox**, players can purchase and sell land, avatars, and other assets as NFTs.

A prime example is **CryptoKitties**, a blockchain-based game that allows users to collect, breed, and trade unique digital cats as NFTs. The success of CryptoKitties has proven the demand for virtual assets and the potential for NFTs to become an integral part of digital commerce.

---

3. Metaverse Startups: New Business Models and Opportunities

The growth of the Metaverse has led to the rise of innovative startups and business models that cater to the unique needs of virtual worlds. Entrepreneurs are capitalizing on the opportunities provided by the Metaverse to create new services, products, and platforms that cater to virtual spaces. From VR/AR development studios to NFT marketplaces and virtual event companies, the Metaverse is fostering a new wave of startups.

- **Virtual Event Services**: With virtual events becoming more popular in the Metaverse, many startups are focusing on creating platforms and tools for hosting virtual conferences, exhibitions, concerts, and social gatherings. These virtual events offer businesses and brands a new way to connect with audiences in immersive environments.
  - o **Example**: **Vatom** is a startup focused on creating a platform for businesses to engage with their

249

customers through **NFT-powered events and experiences**. Vatom's technology allows brands to host branded events in the Metaverse, create virtual merchandise, and reward customers with exclusive digital assets.

- **Metaverse Development Tools**: Another booming business opportunity in the Metaverse is the development of tools and platforms for creating virtual worlds, assets, and experiences. Startups are offering 3D modeling software, game engines, and AR/VR solutions that make it easier for creators to build and monetize their own virtual worlds.

  - ○ **Example**: **Unity Technologies** is a leader in providing game development tools that enable creators to build immersive experiences for the Metaverse. Startups like **Spatial** are offering VR/AR collaboration tools to help businesses create virtual workspaces and meetings.

- **NFT Marketplaces and Virtual Goods Platforms**: As the demand for virtual goods and NFTs continues to rise, new platforms are emerging that specialize in the buying, selling, and trading of digital assets. These platforms cater to artists, game developers, and collectors, providing a marketplace where virtual goods can be exchanged for cryptocurrency or fiat money.

o **Example**: **OpenSea** is one of the most popular NFT marketplaces, allowing users to buy and sell digital art, collectibles, and virtual goods. Startups in the NFT space are also focusing on **virtual fashion**, **virtual real estate**, and **music**, where NFT-based assets can be traded across various Metaverse platforms.

4. Challenges and Risks in Metaverse Business

While the Metaverse offers incredible opportunities, there are several challenges and risks that businesses need to consider before diving into this space.

- **Legal and Regulatory Issues**: As the Metaverse continues to grow, governments and regulators are beginning to examine how existing laws apply to virtual spaces. Issues such as **intellectual property** rights, **taxation**, and **data privacy** will need to be addressed. Virtual businesses will need to stay updated on evolving regulations and ensure compliance.

- **Scalability and Infrastructure**: To support a growing Metaverse, businesses must ensure that their platforms can scale to handle millions of users and transactions. The infrastructure needed to support virtual worlds—such as servers, bandwidth, and

251

storage—must be robust and reliable to avoid disruptions in service.

- **Security and Fraud Prevention**: The digital nature of the Metaverse presents new security challenges. Virtual goods, currencies, and NFTs are attractive targets for cybercriminals, and businesses must implement strong security measures to prevent fraud and theft. Ensuring that virtual transactions are secure and that users' data is protected will be critical for building trust in Metaverse platforms.

---

5. Real-World Example: The Purchase of Virtual Land in Decentraland

Decentraland is a blockchain-based virtual world that allows users to buy, sell, and develop virtual land. As a **decentralized** platform, Decentraland uses **Ethereum** blockchain technology to manage transactions and ownership of virtual property. The purchase of virtual land in Decentraland has become a significant investment opportunity, with some properties selling for large sums due to their potential for development and the rising demand for virtual spaces.

- **The Land Rush**: In **Decentraland**, virtual land is divided into parcels, and users can purchase, build on, and monetize these properties. In 2021, the platform saw a surge in virtual real estate sales, with high-profile investors and brands purchasing large tracts of land to host virtual events, build commercial spaces, or create immersive experiences.

- o **Example**: **Tokens.com**, a virtual real estate investment firm, purchased a plot of land in Decentraland for $2.4 million in 2021. The company intends to use the land to host virtual fashion shows, luxury brand experiences, and art exhibitions, capitalizing on the growing interest in virtual luxury goods and experiences.

Conclusion

The business opportunities in the Metaverse are vast and growing rapidly, from virtual real estate investments and digital goods marketplaces to Metaverse-related startups and virtual event services. As the Metaverse continues to develop, new business models and revenue streams will emerge, offering exciting prospects for entrepreneurs, developers, and investors alike.

Real-world examples like the **purchase of virtual land in Decentraland** and the success of virtual goods in platforms like **Fortnite** and **Roblox** demonstrate the significant commercial potential of the Metaverse. As technology continues to evolve and more users enter virtual worlds, businesses that embrace the opportunities presented by the Metaverse will be well-positioned to succeed in this new digital frontier.

In the next chapter, we will explore **marketing and branding in the Metaverse**, focusing on how companies can create effective marketing strategies and brand experiences within these virtual worlds.

CHAPTER 26

ETHICAL AND SOCIETAL IMPACTS OF THE METAVERSE

Overview: The Societal Implications of the Metaverse, Such as Data Privacy, Economic Inequality, and Digital Addiction

As the Metaverse continues to develop and expand, it brings with it significant societal implications that require careful consideration. While the Metaverse promises exciting opportunities for innovation, social interaction, and economic growth, it also presents ethical challenges that can affect users, businesses, and society at large. Issues such as **data privacy**, **economic inequality**, **digital addiction**, and **social isolation** are becoming increasingly important as virtual worlds become more integrated into our daily lives.

In this chapter, we will explore the ethical and societal impacts of the Metaverse, discussing both the potential benefits and risks that come with the rise of these digital spaces. We will delve into real-world examples such as the debates surrounding **user privacy** and **data security** in platforms like **Facebook Horizon** and **Roblox**, highlighting the need for responsible development and thoughtful regulation.

255

1. Data Privacy and Security in the Metaverse

One of the most pressing ethical concerns in the Metaverse is **data privacy**. Virtual worlds collect vast amounts of data from users, including personal information, behavioral patterns, and even biometric data (such as eye tracking and physical movements). As users spend more time in the Metaverse, the amount of personal information shared and stored in these digital environments grows exponentially.

- **Privacy   Concerns**:
  In the Metaverse, users' activities, preferences, and interactions are constantly being tracked and analyzed by platform operators. This raises concerns about how this data is collected, stored, and shared with third parties. The potential for **surveillance** and the misuse of personal data is a critical issue that needs to be addressed as the Metaverse evolves.
  - **Example**: **Facebook Horizon**, Meta's virtual social space, has been criticized for its data collection practices. The platform collects detailed data on users' interactions, physical movements, and even facial expressions while users are immersed in VR environments. Critics argue that this data could be used to create highly targeted advertisements, or worse, could be

256

exploited in ways that compromise users' privacy and security.

- **Data Security Risks**: With an increasing amount of personal data being stored within virtual platforms, ensuring the **security** of that data becomes crucial. Hackers and cybercriminals could exploit vulnerabilities in the Metaverse's infrastructure to steal user data, commit fraud, or engage in other malicious activities. This poses significant risks to both users and businesses operating within virtual worlds.

  o **Example**: **Roblox**, a popular gaming platform with a vast Metaverse-like experience, has faced issues related to data security. In 2020, the platform was scrutinized for its handling of user data and the security of young users' information. With millions of children and teenagers using Roblox, privacy and safety measures became a significant concern, prompting calls for more robust data protection practices.

- **Regulation and Standards**: The lack of clear, consistent data privacy regulations in virtual worlds is a major issue. Governments around the world are still grappling with how to regulate data collection and user privacy in the Metaverse. Stronger laws and policies will be required to ensure that companies are held accountable for how they handle user data.

---

2. Economic Inequality in the Metaverse

The rise of the Metaverse also raises concerns about **economic inequality**, as access to virtual worlds, digital assets, and opportunities within the Metaverse may not be equally distributed among all users. As virtual economies grow and digital goods become valuable commodities, the question of who benefits from these new opportunities becomes increasingly important.

- **The Digital Divide**: Not everyone has equal access to the hardware and internet connectivity required to participate in the Metaverse. High-quality VR headsets, powerful computers, and stable internet connections can be expensive, which may exclude lower-income individuals from fully participating in virtual worlds. This digital divide could result in a **two-tiered society** where wealthier individuals can access the Metaverse's most lucrative opportunities, while others are left behind.
  - **Example**: The cost of entry into VR-based platforms like **Meta's Horizon Worlds** or **Oculus Quest** remains high for many users. While Meta offers some lower-cost VR headsets,

the hardware required for an optimal Metaverse experience can still be prohibitive for people in low-income households.

- **Wealth Disparity in Virtual Economies**: As virtual economies grow, the creation, sale, and trade of virtual goods and real estate have become valuable sources of income. However, the profits from these activities are often concentrated in the hands of a few individuals or companies. This could exacerbate existing wealth disparities, as only those with the resources to invest in virtual real estate or digital assets can generate substantial profits.

  o **Example**: In **Decentraland**, virtual land is sold as NFTs, and some plots have sold for millions of dollars. While these assets have generated immense wealth for early investors, they have also created a system where the wealthy can continue to dominate the virtual economy, leaving little opportunity for newcomers to break into the market.

- **Virtual Jobs and Economic Opportunities**: The Metaverse also offers new **economic opportunities**, such as virtual jobs, digital commerce, and virtual service industries. However, there is concern that the economic rewards in the Metaverse may not be equally distributed. Jobs in the Metaverse, such as virtual event hosting or

259

avatar design, could require specialized skills and training that not everyone has access to.

- o **Example**: Virtual world platforms like **Roblox** and **Second Life** offer users the ability to create and sell virtual goods or host events. While these platforms have democratized access to entrepreneurial opportunities, only a small number of users are able to turn these activities into profitable businesses, often due to the need for specific digital skills, tools, and resources.

3. Digital Addiction and Social Isolation

As the Metaverse becomes more immersive, there is growing concern about **digital addiction** and its potential to disrupt social dynamics. The allure of spending extended hours in virtual worlds, where users can escape into fantastical environments or live out idealized versions of their lives, has raised concerns about the psychological impact of Metaverse experiences.

- **Escapism and Addiction**: For some users, the Metaverse may become a form of escapism, allowing them to withdraw from the challenges or discomforts of the real world. While the Metaverse offers opportunities for entertainment, socializing, and creativity, excessive use could lead to **addiction**, with users spending an unhealthy amount of time immersed in virtual spaces and neglecting their physical and social well-being.

- o **Example**: In **Second Life**, there have been instances of players becoming so deeply immersed in the virtual world that they spent large amounts of time there, to the detriment of their physical health, relationships, and professional lives. Similar issues are likely to arise as the Metaverse grows more immersive and accessible.

- **Social   Isolation**: Paradoxically, while the Metaverse offers opportunities for social interaction, it may also contribute to **social isolation**. As users become more immersed in digital spaces, they may prioritize online relationships over real-world interactions, leading to a decline in face-to-face communication and real-life social bonds.

  - o **Example**: In platforms like **VRChat**, where users can interact with others via avatars in immersive virtual spaces, there is a risk that people might substitute virtual relationships for real-life connections. This could result in feelings of loneliness or alienation, especially if individuals become more comfortable in virtual worlds than in their offline environments.

261

- **Impact on Mental Health**: Prolonged exposure to virtual worlds may have unforeseen consequences on mental health. Issues such as **depression**, **anxiety**, and **identity confusion** could arise, especially if users become overly invested in their virtual selves and lose touch with their physical world.

---

4. The Role of Developers in Ethical Metaverse Design

As creators and developers of virtual worlds, there is an inherent responsibility to design the Metaverse in a way that promotes ethical behavior, inclusivity, and fairness. The business opportunities and technological innovations that the Metaverse provides must be balanced with a commitment to social responsibility.

- **Ethical Development**: Developers must be proactive in addressing issues such as data privacy, economic inequality, and user safety. This could involve implementing transparent data collection policies, creating inclusive virtual worlds, and ensuring that the digital economy is accessible to a wide range of users.
- **Inclusivity and Accessibility**: The Metaverse must be designed to be accessible to all, regardless of physical ability, socioeconomic status, or

technical expertise. Developers should strive to create spaces that are inclusive, ensuring that users from diverse backgrounds can participate fully and equally.

- **Creating Safe and Healthy Spaces**: Developers should consider the psychological and social impacts of the Metaverse and implement tools and resources to promote healthy engagement. This includes incorporating tools for self-regulation, providing support for mental health, and ensuring that users can easily manage their time spent in virtual spaces.

5. Real-World Example: Debates Surrounding User Privacy and Data Security in Facebook Horizon and Roblox

Two major platforms—**Facebook Horizon** and **Roblox**—have faced significant scrutiny regarding their handling of user privacy and data security.

- **Facebook Horizon**: As Meta pushes further into the Metaverse with **Horizon Worlds**, concerns about **user data** and **privacy** have arisen. The platform collects a wide range of data from users, including biometric data, voice recordings, and physical movements, raising questions about how this data will be used and who will have access to it. Critics argue that Meta's history of data privacy issues further intensifies these concerns.

- **Roblox**:

  Roblox, a platform heavily used by children and teenagers, has also faced criticism over its data protection practices. The platform has been accused of not doing enough to protect its younger users from online predators or inappropriate content. Furthermore, the virtual economy within Roblox has led to concerns over virtual goods transactions, with some users spending real money on in-game items and currency without fully understanding the consequences.

Conclusion

The Metaverse offers a new frontier of innovation and opportunity, but it also brings significant ethical and societal challenges. As virtual worlds become more integrated into our daily lives, we must carefully consider the **privacy**, **economic**, and **psychological** impacts of these technologies. Developers, businesses, and governments all have a role to play in ensuring that the Metaverse is a space that promotes inclusivity, fairness, and user well-being.

Real-world examples from **Facebook Horizon** and **Roblox** underscore the importance of responsible development, data protection, and ethical decision-making in the creation of virtual worlds. As the Metaverse continues to evolve, addressing these ethical concerns will be critical to ensuring that it becomes a safe, inclusive, and empowering space for everyone.

In the next chapter, we will explore the **future of governance and regulation in the Metaverse**, examining how laws, policies, and ethical guidelines can evolve to keep pace with the rapid growth of virtual spaces.

CHAPTER 27

HOW TO BECOME A METAVERSE DEVELOPER

Overview: Practical Steps for Getting Started in Metaverse Development, Including Learning Key Skills, Using the Right Tools, and Getting Involved in the Community

The Metaverse is a rapidly growing digital space, and as it continues to expand, the demand for skilled developers who can build and shape its future is growing as well. The opportunities for developers to create virtual worlds, games, digital assets, and interactive experiences within the Metaverse are vast and diverse. If you're interested in becoming a Metaverse developer, there are several key steps you can take to get started, including learning the necessary skills, choosing the right development tools, and engaging with the Metaverse community.

In this chapter, we will break down the practical steps to becoming a Metaverse developer. We'll discuss the essential skills you'll need to master, the tools you'll need to use, and how you can get involved in the growing Metaverse ecosystem. We'll also highlight real-world examples, such as becoming a developer for platforms like **Roblox** or building a Metaverse space using

Unreal Engine, to give you concrete examples of how to break into this exciting field.

---

1. Learn the Core Skills for Metaverse Development

Before diving into Metaverse development, it's essential to equip yourself with the right skills that will allow you to design, create, and manage virtual worlds. These skills are largely based on knowledge of 3D modeling, game development, and virtual world building. Here are the key skills to focus on:

- **3D Modeling and Design**: As a Metaverse developer, you'll need to be proficient in 3D modeling and design. This involves creating digital assets like avatars, environments, objects, and textures. 3D modeling is the backbone of any virtual world, and understanding how to design assets that are optimized for real-time rendering in virtual environments is crucial.
  - o **Key Tools**: Blender, Autodesk Maya, ZBrush
  - o **Learning Resources**: Free tutorials, online courses, and 3D modeling communities (e.g., Blender Guru on YouTube, CGMA)
- **Game Development**: A significant portion of Metaverse development revolves around game development principles. You'll need to understand how to create interactive environments, build

gameplay mechanics, and optimize virtual worlds for performance. Game engines like **Unity** and **Unreal Engine** are the go-to platforms for Metaverse development.

- o **Key Tools**: Unity, Unreal Engine
- o **Learning Resources**: Unity's official tutorials, Unreal Engine documentation, free online courses (e.g., Coursera, Udemy)

- **Programming and Scripting**: Developing interactive elements, smart NPCs, and handling virtual transactions requires programming knowledge. Programming languages such as **C#** (for Unity) and **Blueprints** (for Unreal Engine) are essential. Additionally, learning **JavaScript** or **Python** can be beneficial, as they are used in many Metaverse tools and virtual environments.

  - o **Key Languages**: C#, JavaScript, Python
  - o **Learning Resources**: Codecademy, freeCodeCamp, YouTube programming tutorials

- **Blockchain and NFTs**: Since the Metaverse often involves virtual economies and digital assets, understanding blockchain technology and **NFTs** (Non-Fungible Tokens) is increasingly important. You'll need to learn how to integrate blockchain solutions into virtual worlds to handle transactions, ownership, and digital asset creation.

    o **Key Tools**: Ethereum, Solidity, OpenSea API

    o **Learning Resources**: Blockchain development courses, platforms like Coursera or Udemy

- **Virtual Reality (VR) and Augmented Reality (AR)**: As VR and AR are key elements in the Metaverse, understanding how to build experiences in these immersive environments is essential. VR and AR development requires specialized skills in building immersive 3D spaces and handling real-time interactions.

    o **Key Tools**: Oculus SDK, ARKit (for iOS), ARCore (for Android)

    o **Learning Resources**: Oculus developer tutorials, Unity VR development courses

---

2. Choose the Right Development Tools

Once you have a foundational understanding of the key skills, it's important to familiarize yourself with the tools and platforms used in Metaverse development. These tools will help you bring your virtual world to life, from designing environments to implementing interactivity and enabling cross-platform experiences.

- **Unity**:
  Unity is one of the most widely used game engines in the Metaverse and is known for its flexibility and

269

accessibility. It's suitable for creating 3D games and interactive virtual environments, and it has robust support for VR and AR development. Unity also supports the development of blockchain-based assets and can integrate with various NFTs.

- o **Use Cases**: Creating VR/AR experiences, interactive games, virtual worlds
- o **Why It's Important**: Unity's large community and ease of use make it an excellent starting point for Metaverse developers.

- **Unreal   Engine**:
Unreal Engine is another popular game engine known for its high-quality graphics and ability to handle complex environments. It's often used for creating more realistic virtual worlds and immersive environments, making it ideal for high-fidelity Metaverse experiences. Unreal Engine's **Blueprints** system allows developers to create interactive experiences without requiring deep programming knowledge.

  - o **Use Cases**: AAA games, realistic 3D environments, high-fidelity virtual worlds
  - o **Why It's Important**: Unreal Engine is perfect for developers who want to create visually stunning experiences and environments for the Metaverse.

- **Roblox   Studio**:
Roblox Studio is an accessible game development platform that allows developers to create games and experiences for the **Roblox** Metaverse. It's user-friendly, which makes it a great option for beginners, and it provides tools for building virtual worlds, customizing avatars, and monetizing your creations through in-game purchases and virtual goods.
  - o **Use Cases**: Game development for Roblox, virtual worlds, interactive experiences
  - o **Why It's Important**: Roblox Studio is perfect for beginner developers who want to create interactive and engaging virtual worlds without heavy coding.
- **Decentraland   and   The   Sandbox**:
These platforms allow you to create, buy, and sell virtual real estate, build interactive spaces, and develop experiences for users. Both Decentraland and The Sandbox use blockchain to manage virtual assets, enabling developers to create NFTs and sell digital goods within their virtual worlds.
  - o **Use Cases**: Creating virtual worlds, buying and selling virtual real estate, designing virtual shops, hosting virtual events

271

o **Why It's Important**: These platforms are ideal for developers looking to get involved in virtual economies and blockchain-based virtual worlds.

3. Get Involved in the Metaverse Community

The Metaverse is a vast and rapidly evolving space, and becoming a part of the **Metaverse developer community** can help you stay updated, collaborate on projects, and learn from others in the industry. Here's how you can get involved:

- **Join Developer Communities**: Online communities like **GitHub**, **Stack Overflow**, and **Discord** are valuable resources for developers. By joining Metaverse-specific communities, you can exchange ideas, share projects, and get feedback from other developers.

  o **Example**: Many Metaverse platforms, such as **Unity** and **Unreal Engine**, have their own dedicated forums and Discord channels where developers can collaborate, ask questions, and stay up-to-date with the latest industry trends.

- **Contribute to Open-Source Projects**: Many Metaverse projects are open source, meaning anyone can contribute to their development. By contributing to these projects, you not only gain

272

experience but also build your reputation as a Metaverse developer.

- o **Example**: Contributing to an open-source Metaverse project on GitHub or joining a hackathon can help you gain hands-on experience and showcase your skills to the community.

- **Attend Metaverse Conferences and Events**: Participating in Metaverse-related conferences, meetups, and hackathons can help you connect with industry professionals, learn about the latest trends, and gain inspiration for your own projects.

- o **Example**: Events like **The Metaverse Summit** and **NFT.NYC** bring together developers, artists, and entrepreneurs who are building the future of the Metaverse. These events offer valuable networking opportunities and insights into the industry.

- **Follow Industry Leaders and Influencers**: Staying informed about the latest developments in the Metaverse can be achieved by following key influencers and developers in the space. Many industry leaders share insights, tutorials, and project updates on social media and blogs.

- o **Example**: Follow figures like **Tim Sweeney** (Founder of Epic Games) or **Yat Siu** (CEO of

Animoca Brands) to keep up with the evolving landscape of Metaverse development.

4. Real-World Example: Becoming a Developer for Platforms Like Roblox or Building a Metaverse Space on Unreal Engine

To better understand how to break into Metaverse development, let's look at two examples:

- **Becoming a Developer for Roblox**: Roblox is a platform that allows users to create their own games and experiences using **Roblox Studio**. To become a developer for Roblox, start by learning how to use Roblox Studio to create interactive experiences. You can monetize your creations by selling virtual goods or gaining revenue through in-game purchases. Many successful Roblox developers started with simple games and grew their following by building engaging, innovative experiences for Roblox users.

- **Building a Metaverse Space on Unreal Engine**: For developers interested in high-quality graphics and complex virtual environments, **Unreal Engine** provides the tools needed to create sophisticated virtual worlds. You can start by learning Unreal Engine's **Blueprints** system to create interactive experiences without needing extensive programming skills. As you gain experience, you can move on to more advanced programming and incorporate features like multiplayer functionality, blockchain integration, or virtual commerce.

Conclusion

Becoming a Metaverse developer is an exciting and rewarding path that requires dedication, creativity, and a strong understanding of various technologies. Whether you're building virtual worlds, creating digital assets, or developing immersive experiences, there are endless opportunities to contribute to the Metaverse's growth and innovation.

By learning the core skills of 3D modeling, game development, and programming, choosing the right development tools, and getting involved in the Metaverse community, you can position yourself as a key player in this rapidly evolving field. Real-world examples like **Roblox** and **Unreal Engine** show that developers of all levels can get started and make an impact in the Metaverse.

In the next chapter, we will explore **the future of Metaverse development**, looking at emerging technologies, trends, and the potential of the Metaverse to change the way we interact, socialize, and do business in the digital age.

Conclusion

The Metaverse represents a bold and exciting new frontier in the digital landscape, offering boundless opportunities for creativity, innovation, and economic growth. As a platform for virtual worlds, immersive experiences, and digital economies, the Metaverse has the potential to transform how we interact with technology, conduct business, and socialize in both the digital and physical realms. With cutting-edge technologies like **Virtual Reality (VR)**, **Augmented Reality (AR)**, **blockchain**, and **AI**, the Metaverse is already reshaping industries, creating new business models, and opening doors to entrepreneurial ventures that were previously unimaginable.

For developers, this rapidly evolving space presents a world of possibilities, but it also comes with challenges that require dedication, continuous learning, and the ability to adapt to emerging technologies. Becoming a Metaverse developer means mastering a diverse set of skills—from 3D modeling and game development to programming, blockchain integration, and virtual economics. As this digital universe expands, so too do the opportunities for developers to create immersive worlds, interactive experiences, and thriving virtual communities.

In this book, we have explored the key concepts, tools, and techniques necessary to get started in Metaverse development. By learning about virtual world design, development platforms, cross-platform integration, and the ethical implications of the Metaverse, you are now equipped with the foundational knowledge to embark on your journey as a Metaverse developer. From building virtual environments using **Unity** and **Unreal Engine** to exploring new business models in virtual economies and digital goods, the skills you acquire will allow you to contribute to and shape the Metaverse's future.

The Metaverse is still in its early stages, but its growth is exponential. With every new technological advancement and innovative platform, the Metaverse inches closer to becoming a fully interconnected, immersive world where users can work, play, socialize, and trade in ways never seen before. As a developer, you are uniquely positioned to be part of this revolution—building the virtual worlds, digital assets, and social experiences that will define the future of the Metaverse.

So, whether you're just starting out or already deep into your Metaverse development journey, remember that the opportunities are vast. Embrace the challenges, continually expand your skillset, and stay engaged with the Metaverse community to help bring about the next evolution of this exciting digital frontier. The future is immersive, interactive, and boundless, and you have the tools to shape it.

The Metaverse is waiting. It's time to build.